CHINESE CARPETS

CHINESE

贾冠颜

·

查尔斯 罗斯托夫

·

李临潘　章玉和

Harry N. Abrams, Inc.,

CARPETS

By
Charles I. Rostov

and

Jia Guanyan

With

Li Linpan and Zhang H. Z.

Publishers, New York

Frontispiece
■ *Carpet woven in the eighteenth century. Clouds and cranes are silhouetted against a* ■
blue sky, and bats and a trident (ji) also appear. Stylized flowers and vine motifs fill
the rest of the field and the border. Wool pile; cotton warp and weft; Senneh knots, 60
per square inch; 6' 1¼" x 11' 9" (1.86 m. x 3.58 m.). The Textile Museum,
Washington, D.C.

Plate 1 (opposite)
■ *Carpet woven in the nineteenth century in north-* ■
western China. In its general layout, this rug is
a forerunner of modern Chinese carpets. A cen-
tral medallion lies on a rather open field, and a
motif is repeated in each corner. The borders
are richly decorated. The colors here, however
—blues on a gold ground—are fewer and less
subtly modulated than in most contemporary
examples. Wool pile; cotton warp and weft;
Senneh knots; 2' 7½" x 5' 1¾" (0.80 m. x
1.57 m.). Royal Ontario Museum, Toronto,
Canada.

Editor: Ellyn Childs Allison
Designer: Carol Robson

Library of Congress Cataloging in Publication Data
Rostov, Charles I.
    Chinese carpets.
    Bibliography: p.
    Includes index.
    1. Rugs—China.   I. Jia, Guanyan.   II. Title.
NK2883.R67   1983   746.7'51   83-3836
ISBN 0-8109-0785-2

The lines of poetry on page 100, from Michael Sullivan, *Chinese
and Japanese Art*, London, © Grolier, 1965, are reprinted by
permission of Franklin Watts, Publishers, New York

Illustrations © 1983 Harry N. Abrams, Inc.
Published in 1983 by Harry N. Abrams, Incorporated, New York

Printed and bound in Japan

Sockchin Hall, Taersi, Xi'ning, Qinghai. See Plate 33.

Contents

Plate 2 (preceding pages)

■ *Detail of a carpet woven in Xinjiang in the late eighteenth century or early nine-teenth century. The central field is filled with pomegranate trees and surrounded by stripes of rich color alternating with bands of rosettes. Silk pile; cotton warp and weft; Senneh knots, c. 90 per square inch. The entire carpet measures 6' 10" x 13' 11" (2.08 m. x 4.24 m.). The Metropolitan Museum of Art, New York. Gift of James F. Ballard. The James F. Ballard Collection, 1922.* ■

FOREWORD

Among the groups of oriental rugs, those made in China are something of an enigma. Their coloring, their motifs, and the place they hold within the culture that created them are dramatically different from those of the Middle East. They have fascinated the collector, and alongside their better-known cousins from Turkey, Iran, the Caucasus, and Central Asia, they have held a respected place within the great rug collections of many museums and individuals.

Much has been written about Chinese carpets, particularly the antique and semi-antique examples. In most instances, however, it has been the eye of the Western connoisseur that has been turned on this material—in admiration and serious study, to be sure, but without the advantage and insight that would come from collaboration with Chinese scholars. Charles Rostov, whose longstanding association with the People's Republic of China has made him sensitive to the need for such collaboration, has undertaken in this book to present a rich and comprehensive treatment of Chinese carpets. Blending the views of East and West, and utilizing sources not previously available to Western writers, Mr. Rostov and his Chinese coauthors trace the history of Chinese rugs from the beginnings of carpet weaving, through the seventeenth, eighteenth, and nineteenth centuries, when the most revered and avidly collected examples were produced, and up to the present day.

For indeed the tradition continues, and while modern Chinese rugs are distinctly different in structure and often in decoration from their earlier prototypes, they have also found a ready market and have had an interesting development in their own right.

Both the steadily increasing interest in old Chinese rugs and the growing numbers of new ones imported into the United States assure the timeliness of this unique publication.

PATRICIA L. FISKE
Director
The Textile Museum,
Washington, D.C.

Plate 3

Carpet woven in Xinjiang in the early nineteenth century. This beautiful old carpet is decorated with a typical Xinjiang medallion containing four rosettes and four small circles. The overall design, however, is unusual. Four borders form the boundaries of the main field. The innermost is drawn with a ruyi *cloud motif; the next has a T-form meander pattern; in the third, diagonal bands enclose the* wan *symbol, representing the wish for ten-thousandfold happiness. The outer border lends a quiet touch to an otherwise active pattern. The colors were probably once brighter and have softened and mellowed with age. Wool pile; cotton warp and weft; Ghiordes knots, 30 per square inch; 4' 8" x 7' 5" (1.42 m. x 2.26 m.). The Textile Museum, Washington, D.C. Gift of Jerome and Mary Jane Straka.*

PREFACE

Interest in the Chinese people grew enormously in the West after the People's Republic of China was founded in 1949, and it has taken quantum leaps since 1972, when the United States opened relations with China. It is my hope that the following pages will stimulate and in some small measure add to our readers' knowledge about this vast country and its ancient culture.

My first postwar contact with China came in August 1972, when, in response to my letter written three weeks earlier, I received a cable from Beijing that read in part, "We welcome Mr. and Mrs. Rostov visit Beijing at beginning of September. Please cable your confirmation." That exciting communication initiated one of the most thrilling travel experiences imaginable. Warmly received by our Chinese hosts, my wife and I were conducted through Shanghai, Tianjin, Beijing, and Guangzhou (Canton) with a hospitality beyond compare. Many of those hosts have become our good friends.

I have since been privileged to travel through large parts of China and to visit carpet production centers in Shanghai, Tianjin, Beijing, Hangzhou, Nanjing, Suzhou, Chongqing, and other areas. Recently I have visited ancient centers of manufacture in the northwest, in Gansu Province and in Xinjiang Autonomous Region, where I was exposed to the culture of minority peoples, many of whom are carpet weavers in the old traditions of northwest China. With my wife and son, I have followed the ancient Silk Route—traveled nearly two thousand years ago

by the armies of the Han emperor Wudi, in the sixth century by the Chinese Buddhist monk Xuan Zang, and, much later, by Marco Polo en route to the court of Kublai Khan. The unforgettable experience of visiting the Buddhist caves at Binglingsi on the Yellow River and Bezeklik in the Taklamakan Desert, as well as the oasis of Turfan (Qoco) and the old city of Kaocheng gave us an infinitely greater understanding of China's history. Wherever I have gone, local carpet experts have been most helpful in explaining regional methods of production.

Since my first trip to China in 1972, I have been impressed by the extraordinarily fine workmanship achieved in all areas of production, from the careful spinning and dyeing of yarn, to skilled hand-knotting of the pile, to the carving and finishing of each piece. Unsurpassed technical skill and continual monitoring guarantee floor coverings of the highest quality. Chemical washing produces a finish with such luster that a layman might mistake wool rugs for silk.

I have long felt that a truly comprehensive book should be written about these exquisite carpets and the history of their manufacture. The topic has fascinated me for many years and I have been impressed by the warm interest, not only among collectors, museum experts, and scholars, but in the large circle of enthusiasts who purchase Chinese carpets and find them luxurious and durable, an investment in beauty and quality.

This book was written jointly with my good Chinese friends Mr. Jia Guanyan,

Mr. Li Linpan, and Mr. Zhang H. Z. Their research, and especially their knowledge of the history of their country, of the techniques of carpet making, of symbolism, and of many other subjects has been invaluable. Much of our information has come from historical records and from the publications of archaeological expeditions. However, some of the stories about carpets have been handed down through the centuries; we cannot prove that they are true, but they have the imprimatur of antiquity and we felt we should include them here.

The interpretation of a system of symbols handed down through the millennia is fraught with danger and often becomes subjective. It is particularly difficult for a foreigner to undertake such a task, and in general I have accepted the interpretations of my Chinese colleagues, avoiding any special comment of my own.

The words "pattern" and "design" have such similar meanings that we decided to use them interchangeably. Usually in our text "design" means the overall look; "motif" means an individual figure or symbol; and "pattern" means a grouping of motifs.

In the world of hand-knotted rugs and carpets, the word "carpet" usually refers to pieces 6 by 9 feet or larger; pieces 4 by 6 feet or smaller are referred to as "rugs." In American usage, however, a carpet is a permanently installed floor covering extending from wall to wall, whereas a rug is a finished piece that takes a dignified place on the floor, quietly or boldly, as an important contributor to the decor. For this reason, because this book will be read in countries where terminology varies, we have decided to use "carpet" and "rug" interchangeably.

Many people in the United States have helped, counseled, and encouraged us. We are particularly indebted to Patricia L. Fiske, Director of the Textile Museum in Washington, D.C., for her interest and guidance; to Jean Mailey, Curator of the Textile Room at the Metropolitan Museum of Art, New York, for her encouragement; to M. A. France for her help in the early stages of preparing the manuscript; to Gene Rostov, my son, for photographs of various stages of rug production that he took during many trips to China; to my secretary, Doris Henkin, for her assistance throughout many months of research, writing, and fact checking; and to Daisy Kwoh of the Asia Society, New York, for checking the romanized spellings of Chinese words.

We would also like to thank Leta Bostelman, managing editor at Abrams, and the project director of our book, for giving us the benefit of her expertise in many aspects of book production; and to our editor, Ellyn Allison, whose work has been indispensable.

Above all, I myself am grateful to my wife, Dorothy, who accompanied me on many visits to China, and without whose patience, forbearance, and encouragement this book could not have been completed.

CHARLES ROSTOV
Scarsdale, New York

Carpet woven in the nineteenth century. The Textile Museum, Washington, D.C.
Detail of Plate 106.

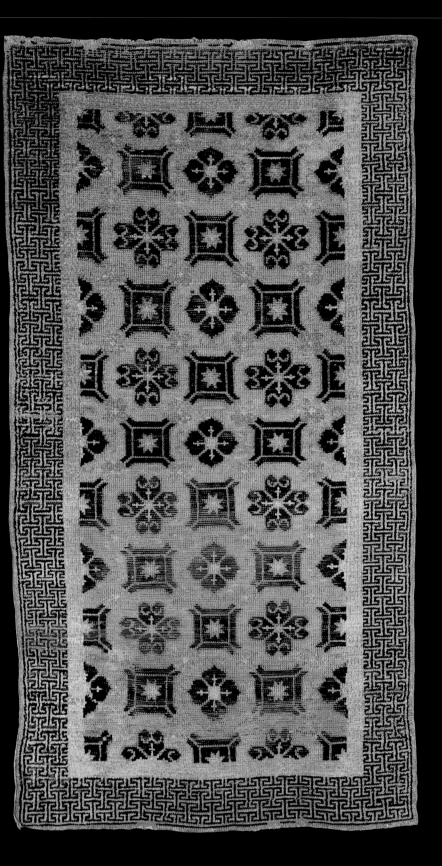

Plate 4

Xinjiang carpet of unusual design woven in the nineteenth century. A lattice of black rectangles joined by rosettes and enclosing stylized floral forms creates a richly decorative effect, enhanced by the heavy fret border. Silk pile; cotton warp and weft; Senneh knots, 42 per square inch; 3' 2" x 5' 10" (0.96 m. x 1.78 m.). The Textile Museum, Washington, D.C. Gift of Jerome and Mary Jane Straka.

PREFACE

For many years I and my colleagues —Mr. Li Linpan, Director of the Tianjin Carpet Research Institute, and Mr. Zhang H. Z., a scholar and linguist— planned to write a book on the subject of Chinese carpets. The topic is fascinating and very broad. To cover it adequately has taken a decade of research, much travel across the vast territory of China, and, with our good friend Mr. Charles Rostov, three years of writing, verification, and translation into English.

This book has been very much a joint venture. To our knowledge, it is the first of its kind written together by Chinese and American experts, as well as the first to draw extensively on Chinese sources. Such international coauthorship has smoothed the difficulties of translation and, we feel, has enriched the content of the book.

In translation poetry tends to lose the most. Its subtleties and lyric qualities tend to disappear in a foreign context. We are indebted to Mr. Zhang for his skillful rendering into English of much of the Chinese poetry quoted here.

We should point out that all the facts —including the dates—in this study are based on Chinese sources. From the beginning, we determined to follow Chinese scholarship, even when it disagreed with Western interpretations.

In endeavors of this nature, the help of others is indispensable. In his Preface, Mr. Rostov has named some of the people in the United States to whom we are indebted. On the Chinese side, I should like to mention Mrs. Gao Tangmin, whose beautiful line drawings fill these pages, and Mr. Liu Shiguang, who has made his fine photographs of carpets and of Chinese buildings and landscapes available to us.

There is a Chinese proverb that translates, "Cast a brick in anticipation of receiving a jade in return." As at last we send this book out into the world of art and literature, we look forward to receiving many valuable ideas from our readers.

JIA GUANYAN
Beijing

Plate 6

Painting in the Palace Museum, Beijing, by Gu Kaizhi, an artist of the Eastern Jin Dynasty (317–420 A.D.). The duke of Wei is sitting on a carpet talking to his duchess, who is seated on several layers of carpeting.

Plate 5 (opposite)

Carpet woven during the second half of the nineteenth century in Hetian (Khotan), Xinjiang. Typical of rugs from this region are the triple medallion pattern, the main border pattern, and the rosettes of the inner border. Unlike the Hetian rug shown in Plate 52, the knots used are the usual Senneh knots (42 per square inch). Wool pile; cotton warp; wool weft; 6' 9⅞" x 13' 7¾" (2.08 m. x 4.17 m.). The Textile Museum, Washington, D.C. Gift of Jerome and Mary Jane Straka.

1. HISTORY

Plate 7

■ *Carpet woven in the nineteenth century. The unusual pattern of this striking piece suggests that it served a special purpose. We believe it was used as a cover for the coffin of an important person. Wool pile; cotton warp and weft; Senneh knots, 67 per square inch; 9' 6⅛" x 5' 8⅛" (2.90 m. x 1.73 m.). The Textile Museum, Washington, D.C.* ■

The Yangshao Age

Much of China's early history, like that of other areas of the world, exists only in a well-kept tradition of myth and legend that is oral, written, or visualized in symbols. As such, it is shrouded in mystery and subject to differing interpretations by serious observers, who demand "hard" archaeological evidence to prove the stories told of the past.

How ancient is Chinese civilization? Inscriptions on thousands of slips of bamboo, compiled much later by Confucian scholars into the Five Classics (see Appendix I), describe city-states that flourished at an indeterminate time before China's earliest dynasty, the Xia (twenty-first century B.C. to seventeenth century B.C.). In this ancient civilization, ruled by a succession of princes, they wove silk, developed a written language, forged weapons of bronze, and rode to war in chariots.

This civilization was considered legendary in the absence of solid proof to the contrary. But dramatic finds by archaeological expeditions in the 1950s and 1960s have proved that ancient cultures existed in what is now called the Yangshao Age.

The story of the Yangshao people lies preserved in the heavy loess deposits in various parts of Asia, particularly along the Yellow River (Huanghe) Basin. The loess provides a calendar of climate and geological events that covers more than two million years.

One of the earliest "hard proofs" was the discovery of the city of Banpo (半坡) near present-day Xi'an (Shaanxi Province). This civilization has been dated about 4000 B.C. More than two hundred families lived in Banpo in forty-six houses, all with entrances facing south to avoid the glacial winds. Two hundred storage pits were built for wheat and millet, and a ditch was dug around the northern side of the settlement to keep the wandering dogs and pigs of the city from getting into the fields.

The Banpo people slept on woven grass mats placed on pounded earth platforms. Animal skins and heavy

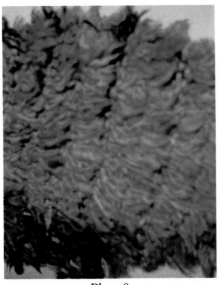

Plate 8
■ *Fragment of wool fabric, perhaps* ■ *very. primitive hand-knotting, dating from about 4000 B.C., discovered near the Normhong River, Tsaidam Basin. Qinghai Museum, Xi'ning, Qinghai.*

woolen textiles kept them warm, and they sewed their clothing with fine needles crafted from bone. Their tools were well designed: stone axes, adzes, and dibbles to make holes for seeds display their skills at agriculture, and arrowheads, fishhooks, and sinkers display their ability at hunting and fishing.

No rug fragments were found at Banpo that would tell us for certain that the people wove rugs, mattresses, or bedding. Rugs and carpets are less durable than bronze, jade, or human bones, and they have not survived as well as objects made of more lasting materials. Archaeologists have speculated on incomplete evidence that felt rugs or animal skins were used, but not necessarily woven pile carpet. One thing is certain, though. When the ancient books use the words "woolen mat," they refer to something made of woolen yarn that was used as a mat or mattress.

Everything about the climate and geography, and the level of the people's art and skill with animal husbandry and tools suggest that they produced wool textiles and mats. By 4000 B.C., herds grazed on the vast northern ranges of grassland surrounded by the mountain ranges of Yin, Tian, Qilian, Kunlun, Himalaya, and Altai, and in the Pamir Highlands. Already the Yangshao people had domesticated not only the pig and the dog, but the ox, goat, horse, and sheep. These animals provided food, a medium of barter and exchange, and a source of wool and hair.

Stone and clay spindles have been excavated throughout the north, and presumably the nomad tribes spun yarn for weaving primitive textiles for clothing and mats. What we know as carpets, to cover a floor, were most likely then used for mattresses or seats.

In 1960, a team of Chinese archaeologists excavating a Neolithic site (c. 4000 B.C.) on a bank of the Normhong River, in the central region of the Tsaidam Basin, found some fragments of coarse woven wool fabric, one piece of which resembles very primitive hand-knotting (Plate 8). These fragments are now in the Qinghai Museum in Xi'ning, Qinghai Province. Study revealed that they were woven by the Qiang natives of the western part of China.[1] Well-preserved by the dry climate of that region, the pile fragment still retains its original colors: yellow, red, brown, and blue.

The discoveries at Banpo surprised the archaeological community, introducing a much earlier date for a highly developed, flourishing city than had previously been supposed. The finding of the Normhong fragment was equally surprising, suggesting that the Chinese pile carpet originated in very early times indeed.

The Shang Dynasty:
17TH Century B.C.–11TH Century B.C.

Guo Moruo, former President of the Academy of Sciences of the People's Republic of China, has stated that the Stone Age cultures of the Yangshao period and before were based on a cultural structure he calls "primitive commune." He claims that these maternal, clan-oriented communes ended with the Shang Dynasty, when great improvements in agricultural production created surpluses of food which, in turn, created a wealthy class of aristocrats capable of owning both land and slaves.

Under the monarchical Shang government a "slave society" arose, with the king as the largest land- and slaveowner. At this time, the people had no great religious leaders or established teachings to follow. They used "oracle bones"—the shoulder blades of cattle and shells of tortoises carved with inscriptions—to communicate with the mysterious powers ruling the tumultuous landscape out of which they had forged a civilization. They relied upon their ancestors, charms, superstitions, and symbols. In the world beyond the Himalayas, Egypt celebrated its 18th, 19th, and 20th dynasties, Moses led the Hebrews across the Red Sea, and the Mycenaean kings conquered Troy.

Oracle bones were first discovered by Chinese peasants digging ditches in their fields. Believed to be dragon bones with medicinal value, they were bought in large quantities by Chinese druggists, who pulverized them and sold the powder for use under certain medically prescribed formulas. In the 1880s these excavations came to the attention of Chinese archaeologists, who recognized the historical value of the bones.

More than 100,000 pieces of inscribed bone and shell have yielded 4,800 different words, 1,700 having recognizable meaning. One third of the 4,800 words were hieroglyphs, and the other two thirds associatives— words formed by combining two or more elements or roots, each with its own meaning, to create the new meaning. For example, the figure of a woman next to the figure of a male child, presumably her son, conveys the meaning "good."

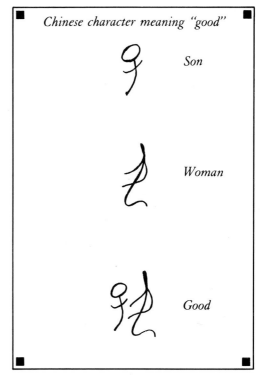

Chinese character meaning "good"

Son

Woman

Good

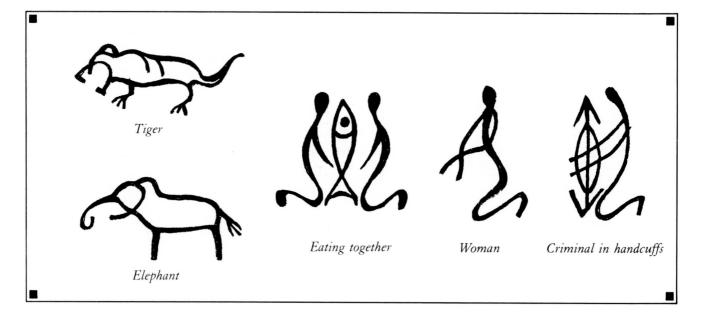

Tiger

Elephant

Eating together

Woman

Criminal in handcuffs

The inscriptions on bones record the lives of the people dwelling in Stone Age and Bronze Age cities. From these words can be gleaned an understanding of their social philosophy as well as information on how they worked, fished, waged wars, and herded cattle. A figure with a long trunk, for instance, tells us that they were familiar with elephants.

One of the words designates a woven mat. It is a herringbone design framed with an oblong border, suggesting that mats were made of flattened stalks of straw or reeds woven in a herringbone pattern. At this time, people sat on mats laid on the floor. The pictograms shown below can be read as follows:

We also know that this ancient people had a word for spindle. It consists of three parts, the figures of an implement (the spindle itself) and a ball of yarn above the figure of a hand.

The words "spindle" and "mat" suggest very strongly that people living in China some 4,000 years ago were capable of weaving mats of twisted yarn. As we shall see, physical evidence for this exists as well.

In the Shang and early Zhou dynasties, writing became an important achievement. Their folk songs were later collected in *Maoshi*, or *Book of Odes*, and today poetry aids archaeology in determining when certain objects were used and for what purpose. Thus began the description of the early history of rugs and carpets.

Woven mat

Woven mat in a cave

Man going to bed
in a shelter or room

Man in bed

Man sitting on a woven mat

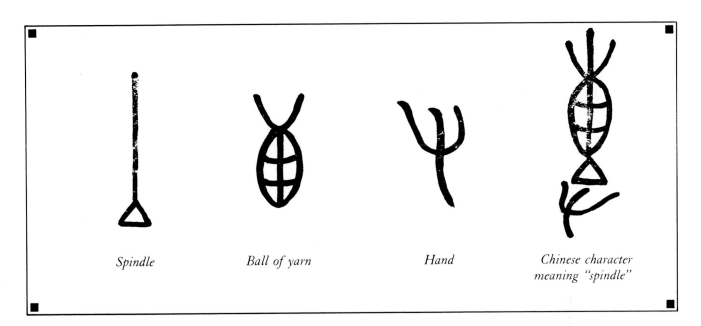

Spindle   *Ball of yarn*   *Hand*   *Chinese character meaning "spindle"*

The Zhou Dynasty:
11TH Century B.C.–221 B.C.

The tumultuous Shang Dynasty, both a golden age and a dark age of slavery and human sacrifice, was brought to an end about 1050 B.C. by the Zhou people, invaders from the west.

The Zhou Dynasty is divided into two eras: the Western Zhou (eleventh century B.C.–771 B.C.), with its capital at Haojing (near present-day Xi'an) in Shaanxi Province; and the Eastern Zhou, which is subdivided into the Spring and Autumn Period (770–476 B.C.) and the Warring States Period (475–221 B.C.). In 770 the capital was moved eastward to Luoyi (present-day Luoyang) in Henan Province.

The conquest of the Shang Dynasty took about twenty years, and when it was accomplished, the Zhou, essentially a pastoral, agricultural people, assimilated and absorbed the Shang political practices and their art. Among Chinese historians the stage of development of Western Zhou society is still a matter of controversy, many seeing it as the beginning of feudalism, others maintaining that it was still a slave society. The new patrons of the arts were local aristocrats, wealthy merchants, and landowning families who collected tribute from serfs living in their fiefdoms.

Surviving members of the Shang court were allowed to live in one small area.[2] Captured prisoners included skilled laborers, whose value was not lost upon the Zhou. They were organized as Baigong (百工), the "Hundred Workers," and in the Thirteen Classics, another compilation of Confucian literature, it is recorded that officials "in charge of skins and pelts" were appointed by the sovereign to engage in collecting wool and hair to make felts in preparation for use in state affairs.[3]

The Zhou used felted material as carpets and rugs because its closer, thicker texture was good in keeping the western and northern cold off the floor. In another Classic, *Shangshu* (尚书),[4] the story is recorded that a Sichuan governor gave a tribute of wild animal skins to the emperor, who decreed that "the Hundred Workers make furs from the skins and floor coverings from the hair and wool." In these writings, the word *ji* (罽) was used, which means woolen materials made of colorfully dyed yarn for blankets or coverings.

From all this it may be reasonable to conclude that some of the Hundred Workers constituted a carpet workshop owned by the Zhou government. It is also known that trade in carpets was sponsored by the nobles and the imperial family.

These references in the Classics give the earliest, very brief account of carpet making. Coupled with the Normhong carpet fragment recovered from the Neolithic strata of the earth, the evidence leads us to believe that "carpets" were produced in China in very ancient times.

■

The Qin Dynasty:
221 B.C.–207 B.C.

Laozi
Modern copy of a traditional portrait

Toward the end of the Zhou Dynasty were born China's first great philosophers. Kong Qiu, known in the West as Confucius (c. 551 B.C.–479 B.C.), played a very important role in summarizing and spreading academic knowledge. There were many other philosophical schools, including those led by Modi, Laozi, Zhuangzi, and Shang Yang. The school of Laozi and Zhuangzi eventually became the Taoist religion but, like the others, was also a purveyor of political thought. Unlike the Greeks, whose political ideas did not extend beyond the city-state, the Chinese were developing a vision of empire that was to become a reality in the Qin Dynasty.

After more than 250 years of chaos in the Warring States Period, the death throes of the Zhou Dynasty, a conqueror emerged who established the first Chinese empire. He was Shihuangdi, founder of the short Qin Dy-

Confucius
Copy of a painting made in the Tang Dynasty
(618–907 A.D.) by Wu Daozi

nasty, and famous forever as the ruler who unified China between 230 B.C. and 221 B.C.

Plate 9

■ *The Chinese frequently turn to ancient patterns for inspiration, thus complicating for* ■
modern scholars the dating of carpets. In this rug woven in Tianjin in 1981, however, it is
patterns on ancient bronze ware, rather than older carpet designs, that are replicated.
Depicted are the skirmishes and battles of the Warring States Period. Wool pile; cotton
warp and weft; Senneh knots, 120-line quality; 3' x 5' (0.92 m. x 1.53 m.).

He developed a centralized bureaucratic military government at Xianyang (Shaanxi Province) and held his vast new empire in control by various means, including building a succession of ambitious engineering projects. He standardized weights and measures, including axle width so all Chinese vehicles could travel along the same rutted roads. He built new roads and canals, and completed the Great Wall to keep out the ever-threatening nomads from the north. Many earlier states had built walls to keep out the northern barbarians, but in 214 Shihuangdi connected them into one for-

tification 4,150 miles (6,700 kilometers) long.[5] He was great in these respects, yet he was a tyrant who burned books on all subjects but medicine, agriculture, and divination. He buried scholars alive and would not tolerate dissent.

Shihuangdi died in 210 B.C. and the united Qin Empire did not long survive. A coup d'etat took place among his heirs in the royal house and the second son assumed the throne. Later, rebellion broke out and the empire crumbled in 206 B.C. The Qin capital of Xianyang was captured by the army led by Liu Bang (256 B.C.–195 B.C.), a petty officer from a peasant family.

Plate 10

Antique Finish carpet made in Inner Mongolia in 1979 on the theme of the Six Steeds of the Zhao Mausoleum (see Chapter 2). The pile in this type of carpet is dyed with vegetable dyes, which give it a mellow look reminiscent of ancient rugs. Wool pile; cotton warp and weft; Senneh knots, 90-line quality; 4' x 6' (1.22 m. x 1.83 m.).

The Han Dynasty:
206 B.C.–220 A.D.

The Qin Dynasty paved the way for the mighty Han Dynasty, a rich, relatively peaceful period. The philosophies of the Zhou became accepted as religions; scientific discoveries advanced. This period of tremendous intellectual activity was enriched by new information from the outside world on art, science, literature, music, industry, and sport gained through conquest and also through trade along the Silk Route, as we will shortly see.

There was an atmosphere of expansion, both intellectual and geographical. Han emperors conquered new enemies and old until the empire stretched across the Asian continent from Tibet and the Tarim Basin, north across Mongolia to Korea, south to the rich port of Canton (now Guangzhou), and west to Afghanistan, where the Han even exacted tribute from the Kushan kingdom. So great was this empire that since then the Chinese have always called themselves the "men of Han," or the "Han people."

The story of how Liu Bang, the Peasant General, outsmarted and outfought the aristocrat Xiang Yu for possession of the imperial throne after the defeat of the Qin is the topic of countless stories, legends, and tales, and a favorite subject in scrolls and paintings.[6]

After he became emperor in 202 B.C., Liu Bang's major problem was the Xiongnu, or Huns, north of the Great Wall. He expanded the empire in all directions to include more states, but the Xiongnu swept down the Yellow River plain and trapped him in a fortified town. Liu was forced to conclude a treaty giving the Xiongnu large tribute in silks, wine, grain, and food, and even a Chinese princess for their chieftain to marry. It was not the first humiliating bargain the Xiongnu were to drive with various Chinese rulers.

The second great Han emperor was Wudi ("Martial Emperor"), who ruled from 140 B.C. to 87 B.C. A man of extraordinary energy and military enterprise, he pushed China's borders far to the south and west. An intriguing observation on Wudi's character has come down to us: apparently the Martial Emperor hated the clattering noise of chariots and horses, and ordered the ground to be covered with felt carpets and sheets, even in the open air.

Searching for allies against the Xiongnu, Wudi sent envoys to the Yuezhi in Afghanistan and to the Wusun north of the Tarim Basin, and these ambassadors to western Asia were sometimes followed by armies. After Wudi's death, Chinese soldiers crossed the Pamirs and in 36 B.C. even confronted Roman legionnaires in Sogdiana(Transoxiana)—for the first and only time.

During Han times trade increased between China and the rest of the world. Great rivers became major transport routes, supplemented by networks of canals. The fabled Silk Route, established by Wudi, extended as far as the shores of the Mediterranean (Plate 16). Important trade began to develop between China and states to the west, including Persia, India, and even Rome. China exported silks, gold, pearls, fine ceramics, jade, and other valuable articles and imported glass, gemstones, curios, furs, and rare birds and animals.

During the Han Dynasty, one practice of defining people's status came to be by the kind of material upon which they sat. The emperor was privileged to sit on a magnificent thick cotton brocade (tijin), dukes and other nobles on fine woven textiles (xiji). In northern China, wool carpets were used by the privileged class as cushions, replacing the older furs and felt. A folk song describes this:

Inviting our guests into the north hall,
On carpets of wool, I sat them all.

Several minor kingdoms in western China produced fine *ji*, woven in a variety of colorful patterns, and multicolored spotted rugs called *banji* were produced in the southwest. But the simple, geometric patterns of Han *ji*, although woven in large numbers, are not comparable in quality to those produced later.

Ancient books occasionally contain records of carpets and carpet making in China. Different names were given to various kinds of carpets since, as the rugs came into being, they were described in writing at different places and different times. Some of the names

Plate 11

Remarkably well preserved despite its great age is this carpet, woven in inland China or Hetian (Khotan) in the early seventeenth century, which may have served as a table cover or kang *cover. An all-over pattern of dragons and double-tailed clouds is bordered by a band of* wan *and bat motifs. Silk pile; silk warp and weft; Senneh knots, c. 156 per square inch; 4' 8" x 3' (1.42 m. x 0.91 m.). The Metropolitan Museum of Art, New York. Rogers Fund, 1908.*

have complicated construction as characters, but most were generally composed on the root *mao* (毛), which means woolen, and the branch expressing where they were laid or used—on earthen beds, or *kangs* (炕),[7] on the floor, or hanging on walls. One of these names, *qushu* (氍 毹), was coined only for pile carpets.

The historical records[8] contain one entry that the influential Grand Marshal Dou Xian (28–92 A.D.) asked Ban Chao (34–102 A.D.), who had been appointed Governor of the Western Territory after his heroic conquest of border districts occupied by the Xiongnu, to sell 700 bolts of silk in variegated colors and 300 bolts of plain-colored silk, and to buy a large lot of Kunduz-Kashgar carpets from the west. Ban Gu (32–92 A.D.), the famous historian and compiler of the *History of the Han Dynasty*, also wrote to Ban Chao, his brother, asking him to "purchase some ten pieces of *ji* in various qualities with eight hundred thousand cash." The historical records also tell us that when the Xiongnu surrendered, "all kinds of carpets, rugs, textiles, tents, felt, furs, and so on were piled up in big heaps as high as mountains." Carpets and other *ji* textiles were a valuable indemnity paid to the victorious side in war.

The Later (Eastern) Han Dynasty (25–220) was never as strong financially, militarily, or administratively as the Earlier (Western) Han had been. China's hold on Central Asia gradually weakened, and after a series of popular revolts the generals became virtually independent warlords, eventually dividing the empire in three. This period, called the Three Kingdoms, was racked by incessant warfare. In the third century, a general of the Wei kingdom succeeded in conquering the kingdoms of Wu and Shu, establishing the Jin Dynasty, which endured a mere 150 years (265–420).

The period from 420 to 589 also rang with the noise of wars and revolutions. During these troubled times there was a resurgence of Taoism, and Buddhism too gained enormous popularity. In 589 China was reunited by the short but important Sui Dynasty (589–618), which paved the way for the mighty Tang Dynasty, much as the Qin had prepared the way for the Han.

Between 220 and 618, there is at least one story relating to carpets. The famous monk Facun from Guangzhou possessed a carpet "with a length of eight *chi* (see Appendix II), and on it were one hundred patterns of various figures." This carpet was well known to the nobility and the elite, and it brought catastrophe to its owner. The villainous son of a governor coveted the valuable carpet and put the monk to death to get it.[9]

Explorers and archaeologists have eagerly searched during the last hundred years for relics that might unveil unknown facts about trade along the Silk Route, working at Dunhuang, Lop Nor, the Altai district, and the Tarim Basin.

One of the earliest modern explorers of this region was Aurel Stein, who in 1904 discovered remains of carpets at the site of the vanished city of Loulan near the "shifting" lake of Lop Nor. These fragments are believed to date from the Han Dynasty.

In 1959, China sent a team of archaeologists to Xinjiang (Uighur) Autonomous Region, where they discovered the ancient site of Niya on the Silk Route, in the desert state of Jingjue, northeast of the now Minfeng County (Plate 13). A large coffin was unearthed containing the corpses of a husband and wife buried during the Western Han Dynasty. On top of the coffin was a fragment of ancient carpet (Plate 14) knotted with wool yarns dyed many colors, on a base of wool warp; the patterned lozenges were woven in a pile height of about three fourths of an inch (twenty millimeters). The yarns were tied every seventh weft in horseshoe knots[10] on single and double warps.

Plate 12
Wooden comb tool (weft dabber), probably dating from the Western Han Dynasty (206 B.C.–24 A.D.), found at Niya by Chinese archaeologists. Xinjiang Museum, Urumqi, Xinjiang.

It is believed that this carpet was fashioned in a method transitional between weaving and knotted-pile making. At the Niya site was also found a wooden comb tool with twenty-two teeth (Plate 12). Apparently it was a weft dabber, used by weavers at that time when knotted-carpet making was in its infancy.[11] The Niya fragment is seeming proof that carpets were indigenous to that region. That piece is so close to the pile carpet of the present day that it may be taken as a forerunner of the Chinese carpet. The Niya fragment is now in the Xinjiang Museum in Urumqi.

The Silk Route made important political, economic, social, and cultural contributions to China. Various religious beliefs had been introduced via this route by the end of the Han Dynasty. Buddhism came from India about 60 A.D. and was accepted by the fifth century and then patronized by the Tang imperial houses. It influenced Chinese hearts and minds more than any other religion, mingling with the Taoism that arose from the writings of Laozi and Zhuangzi. Zoroastrian and Manichaean sects of Christianity came from Persia; from the East Christian Empire came the Nestorians[12]; and from Arabia came Islam.[13]

Plate 13
■ *Ruins of Niya, Taklamakan Desert,* ■
Xinjiang.

Plate 14
■ *Fragment of wool carpet discovered in 1959* ■
at Niya on top of a coffin dating from the
Western Han Dynasty (206 B.C.–24 A.D.).
Xinjiang Museum, Urumqi, Xinjiang.

A Chinese monk, Xuan Zang (596–664 A.D.), spent seventeen years in India studying and preaching Buddhism, having traveled across the Tian and Hindu Kush mountains between 629 and 631 in a quest for the Buddhist scriptures, which he later housed in the Dayan Pagoda ("Big Wild Goose Pagoda") in the capital at Chang'an (modern Xi'an).

The importation of these different religions had a deep influence on Chinese art, not least on rugs and carpets. The Buddhist monasteries were major buyers of rugs to cover their floors, pillars, and seats, and tapestries were also exhibited in their halls.

Already in the Han Dynasty, and on into the Tang, thousands of foreign visitors came to Chang'an to conduct business and to study. According to official records, several thousand

Plate 15

An early nineteenth-century carpet patterned in pale blue, medium blue, and dark blue, this example has a stylized floral and leaf border. Wool pile; cotton warp and weft; Senneh knots; 1' 9¼" x 3' 7½" (0.545 m. x 1.11 m.). Royal Ontario Museum, Toronto, Canada.

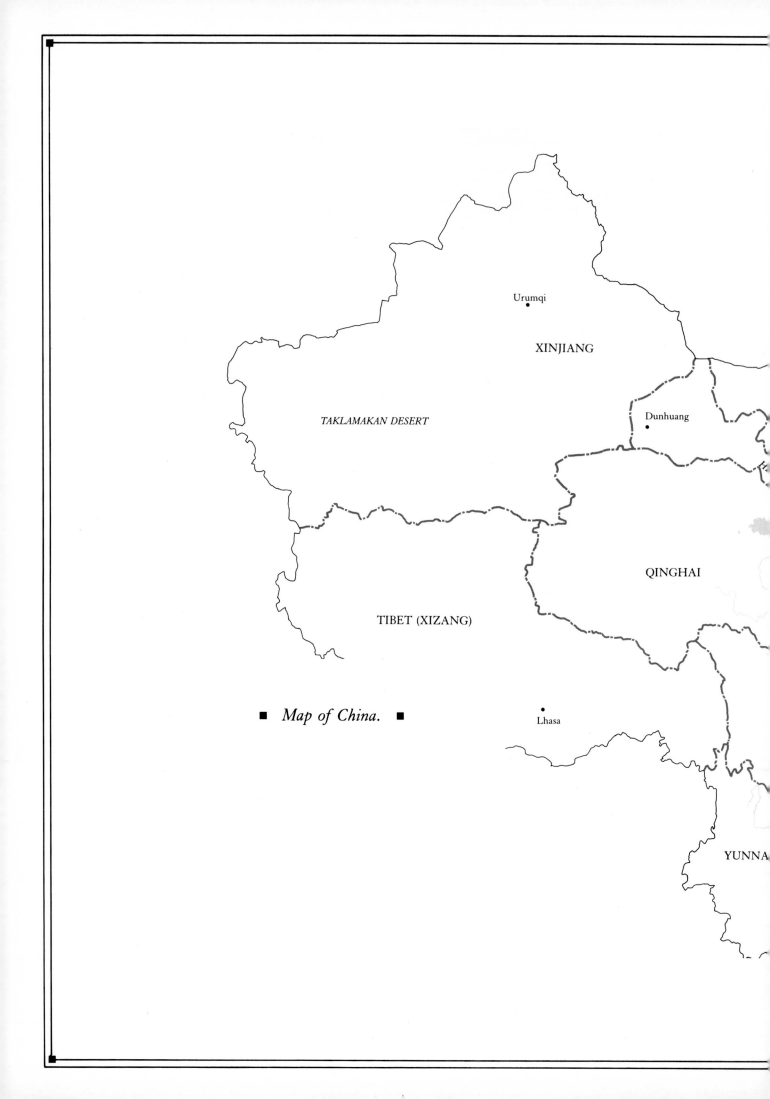

Urumqi

XINJIANG

TAKLAMAKAN DESERT

Dunhuang

QINGHAI

TIBET (XIZANG)

■ *Map of China.* ■

Lhasa

YUNNA

Ili

Urumqi

Be

Tian Mts.

Kucha   Turfan

Karashahr

Aksu

Loulan

Kashgar

L

Pamir Highlands

Taklamakan Desert

Tashkurghan

Yarkand

Dandanuilik   Niya   Charklik

Hetian
(Khotan)

Karakorum Mts.

Kunlun Mts.

Plate 16
■ *Map and view of the Silk Route.* **■**

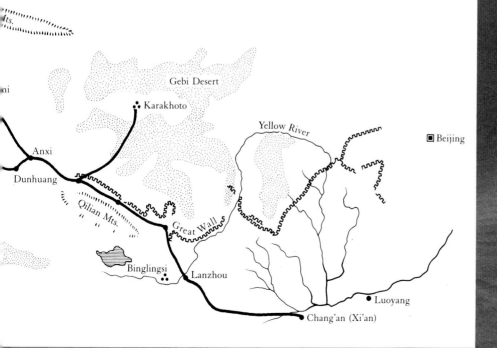

Plate 17

■ *A meander pattern with peonies dec-* ■
orates this seat mat woven in Ningxia
in the eighteenth century. Wool pile;
cotton warp and weft. Whereabouts
unknown.

Plate 18

■ *Detail of a stone carving, from the* ■
Tang Dynasty (618–907 A.D.) with
a design of crockets and tendrils and
a pair of mandarin ducks. Xi'an,
Shaanxi.

Persian merchants stayed in Chang'an during the Han Dynasty, and in the Tang the number swelled to nearly one hundred thousand. Western fashions were accepted by young Chinese people, who copied its elements ardently. Western apparel, Western pastries, and Byzantine textiles became stylish. Nobles and rich families sent these as gifts to one another.

The Silk Route had a profound effect upon the development of Chinese carpet manufacture. Great advances were made in skill and quality as a result of the cultural flow from West to East. Chinese silk weavers learned from Persian textile weavers and succeeded in making Persian damask, a textile woven with wool and cotton yarn. Crocket and tendril motifs (Plate 18) were introduced from the West and the animal-bird continual pattern also appeared at that time.

Similarly some carpets, like the ones from Xinjiang, were influenced by cultural contact along the Silk Route and thus they are related to carpets produced in Persia and the Central Asian countries (Plate 51). However, the designs and symbolism of inland China carpets were derived from sources that are principally Chinese: continual geometric patterns (Plate 28), multi-way figures, meander patterns (Plate 15), and other geometric compositions of flowers and leaves (Plate 17), all of which began in the Han and continued through the Tang, down to the Song and Ming dynasties.

The Tang Dynasty:
618–907

In 618, with the assassination of the Sui emperor Yang Guang (569–618), the Tang Dynasty began. It is regarded as the most brilliant era in China's history, a golden age of art and poetry. Like the Han Dynasty, it was a time of unification and comparative peace, during which a central government was reestablished, lands were redistributed, and religious tolerance was enjoyed. Temples to Confucius were built, the canal system was expanded and improved, and the Tang Code of Law was introduced.

Foreign influence was strong during the Tang Dynasty. Tibet was unified in 607 and Chinese civilization now spread there for the first time. Coming to China was a constant stream of foreign travelers, pilgrims, envoys, and traders who brought new ideas. The Chinese mapmakers achieved much as a result of all these travelers' tales. Printing from wood blocks was developed by 700, arousing an insatiable demand for books. There were new foods, new styles of lettering, and a rebirth of learning. The Tang Dynasty was one of the strongest in Chinese history, and when it fell, many centuries passed before China regained a comparable art and culture.

Carpet making was popularized across the country. The industry benefited by an increase in population and a brisk economy. Government officials and high military officers from Central Asia and Asia Minor served in the Tang armed forces at Chang'an,

the capital, and in many other cities along the Yellow River and the Yangtze (Changjiang) Valley. These and other rich families bought fine carpets of wool and silk. The imperial house was an important customer, requiring large numbers of carpets upon which to conduct its official ceremonies, as well as for household furnishings.

Buddhism became a huge institution during the Tang Dynasty. Records dating from the ninth century mention 4,600 temples, 40,000 shrines, and 260,500 monks and nuns—which would have constituted another large market for carpets (Plate 19). Fearing the growth of this powerful empire within the empire, the emperor Wuzong in 845 ordered the destruction of the temples and shrines and the secularization of the monks and nuns on the grounds that Buddhism was a "foreign" religion, and it was put under the control of the Bureau of Foreign Affairs.[14] But Buddhism had become Chinese by then, and did not disappear.

In 838 the Japanese pilgrim Ennin came to China to study Buddhist sutras. After his return to Japan nine years later, he wrote a diary entirely in Chinese in which carpets are mentioned at least five times. He recounts his participation in an elaborate official ceremony that took place in the open courtyard before the gate to a governor's mansion: all the guests prostrated themselves on carpets before the governor. Although wooden chairs, tables,

■ Plate 19 ■

Details of a painting in the Palace Museum, Beijing, by Lu Lingjia, an artist of the Tang Dynasty (618–907 A.D.). Arhats, Buddhist monks who have attained Nirvana, are seated in armchairs covered with carpets.

Plate 20

■ *Fresco of the Tang Dynasty (618–907 A.D.) on the south wall of Cave 220, Dunhuang,* ■
Gansu, depicting the Buddhist paradise. On gaily colored carpets spread on emerald-green
grass, groups of deities are seated picnic-style.

and raised beds were built from the seventh century on, important ceremonies were still conducted on carpets. Ennin also described an octagonal silk carpet that exactly fit an octagonal marble platform at the Buddhist holy site of Wutaishan in Shanxi Province.

The Tang Dynasty saw important stylistic changes in Chinese art and rug design, largely through the influence of India and Persia. Patterns became more elegant, and more realistic in their representation of actual objects. Paintings and scrolls from this period show designed carpets on floors and seats (Plate 22). In the murals at Dunhuang,[15] painted during the Northern Wei (386–534), Sui, and Tang dynasties, large parties of people eating and dancing are seen on colorful carpets (Plate 20). In the Shoso-in (正倉院), the imperial storehouse at Nara, Japan, there are more than ten thousand valuable relics dating back to the seventh century that include many carpets made in China.

Information about Tang Dynasty carpets can be found in the poetry and stories of the period, and in official

Plate 21

■ *Detail of a blue and gold carpet woven in the nineteenth century. Dragons in profile fill the corners of the field and a front-facing, five-clawed dragon coils in the central medallion. Between narrower borders of geometrical motifs is a wide border with scrolling vines and flowers emblematic of the four seasons. Silk pile; cotton warp; weft of metal threads; Senneh knots, c. 60 per square inch. The entire carpet measures 9' 3" x 13' (2.82 m. x 3.962 m.). The Metropolitan Museum of Art, New York. Gift of William M. Emery, 1963.* ■

Plate 22
■ *Painting in the Palace Museum, Beijing, by Zhou Fang, an artist of the Tang* ■
Dynasty (618–907 A.D.) who specialized in painting women. Here he shows two
ladies and a maid sitting on a carpet.

Plate 23
■ *Young Uighur women in a town along the Silk Route are performing the ritual* ■
"dance of silk." The carpets are in typical Xinjiang designs and colors.

records as well. In "A Scarlet Carpet" (红 线 毯), the great poet Bo Juyi (772–846) tells how the governor of Xuan Prefecture in Anhui Province ordered a silk carpet specially made to win favor from the emperor. In the poem is not only a description of the carpet but something about the market, other carpets, and the way his carpet was made:

A SCARLET CARPET

(My Worry about the Waste of Silkworms and Mulberry Trees)

Selecting the best worms, reeling fine silk,
Boiling them in clear water,
Picking out yarns, choosing strong threads,
Dying them in red color;
Dye them red, redder than the crimson flowers—
Weave the yarns into a carpet for the Imperial Palace.

Palace Fragrant is a hundred-foot-wide hall,
The scarlet carpet is woven for wall-to-wall,
Colored yarns clustered on the downy surface,
Enticed a sensation of flowery fragrance,
The springy piles and the puffy blossoms,
Seemed incapable of sustaining a weight so gross.

On this beautiful textile we saw charming girls who
Sang and danced with graceful steps,
Their silk stockings and embroidered shoes
For a while submerged in the soft piles.

Carpets from Taiyuan are stiff and unsmooth,
Those from Chengdu are thin and lanky,
Couldn't compare with this floor covering
in softness and warmth.

Every Autumn orders are placed on Xuanzhou;
Cudgeling his mind the Governor digs up new patterns,
Thinks himself loyal and is able to do the best.
To carry it to the Palace needs a hundred men,
The carpet is so thick it can't be rolled and packed.

Does Xuan Governor know anything of the fact
That for every ten feet of carpet
A thousand ounces of silk are used?
The ground has no sense of cold
Yet people want the means to keep warm.
Please make fewer floor coverings,
To spare the material for making apparel.

Plate 24
■ *Painting by Liu Jun of the Ming Dynasty* ■
(1368–1644 A.D.), in the Palace Museum,
Beijing. The Song emperor Taizu is seen
visiting his prime minister, Zhao Pu, on a
snowy night, when the carpet they are sit-
ting on must have been a welcome luxury.

The poem compares carpets from Cheng-du (Sichuan) and Taiyuan (Shanxi) to the superior carpets of Xuanzhou (the southeastern area of Anhui Province), evidently the best at that time.

All the arts in the populous districts benefited from the patronage of the urban rich. The popularity of silk carpets shows that carpets had changed from a practical covering for the floor, to keep people warm, to a decorative covering for floor or wall.

In a biography of Emperor Zhong-zong the character traits of a Tang nobleman and his visitor are included in an account of an exceptional carpet. The story goes that Wei Zhi, a noble of the court and kinsman of the empress, fell ill; the chief magistrate's son visited him, and finding every room of Wei's mansion covered with carpet of high quality, he took off his boots before entering the bedroom. Being thrifty and simple, he was unaccustomed to such luxury, and thought the carpet too clean and dear to be trampled by dirty boots. The nobleman must have been a man of high standing and wealth, who spared no money in covering his floors so lavishly.

A great poet of the Tang Dynasty, Du Fu (712–770), wrote this about his friend Zheng Qianyuan, a famous and learned scholar of scanty means:

The fame of talent you have enjoyed
for forty years,
On the cold ground,
you have no carpet to seat your guests.

Murals in the ancient caves and large temples show paintings of Tang carpets in a wide range of colors. Patterns of the carpets made in central China did not have the mystical and abstract motifs of previous ages but instead had a realistic tendency. Most of the patterns show flowers, birds, and animals combined with complicated tangles of crocket and tendril motifs. These patterns are very similar in appearance to stone carvings in northern China and to the flower-bird motifs on silk and satin brocade woven in southern China (Plate 25).

At the beginning of the tenth century the Tang Dynasty, weakened by declining administrative efficiency and loss of military control, fell to one of the commanders of the border regions. The following fifty-three years, a period called the Five Dynasties (907–960), was a time of continual war in northern China. Cities were deserted, the countryside was entirely in disorder, and the population dwindled to 60 percent of its former size. Suffering most was the middle Yellow River Valley, from which people fled to the comparatively peaceful south, where, as a result, economy and culture thrived. The newcomers from the north provided a source of labor for agriculture and the handicraft industries. Household furnishings became widely accessible, but warm temperatures and a damp climate discouraged the use of floor coverings. There were chairs to sit on and wooden beds to sleep in —no need for seat mats or *kang* covers. Carpet making appears to have ceased entirely during this time in South China.

Bo Juyi
A Tang Dynasty poet, author of "A Scarlet Carpet" (page 49). Copy of a portrait in Album of Saints and Men of Literature. *Palace Museum, Beijing, Nanshon Gallery*

Plate 25

Carpet woven in 1980. The motifs include birds, flowers, phoenixes, endless knots, and designs taken from stone carvings; the style suggests Tang Dynasty textiles. Wool pile; cotton warp and weft; Senneh knots, 120-line quality; 6' x 9' (1.83 m. x 2.74 m.).

Plate 26

Painting in the Palace Museum, Beijing, by Hu Huai, an artist of the late Tang Dynasty (618–907 A.D.). Depicted are a group of northern tent dwellers and their Han guest (the man wearing the top hat), who have stopped to rest in a large tent. The chieftain and his guest are sitting on a carpet.

Plate 27

Carpet woven in Tianjin in 1981. Tendril patterns like this one, inspired by the design on a Tang Dynasty stela, were very much in vogue during the Sui and Tang dynasties (589–907 A.D.). Here, spiraling leafy vines set off the main motif of honeysuckle and other flowers. Rugs of this sort were exported westward along the Silk Route. Wool pile; cotton warp and weft; Senneh knots, 120-line quality; 3' x 5' (0.92 m. x 1.52 m.).

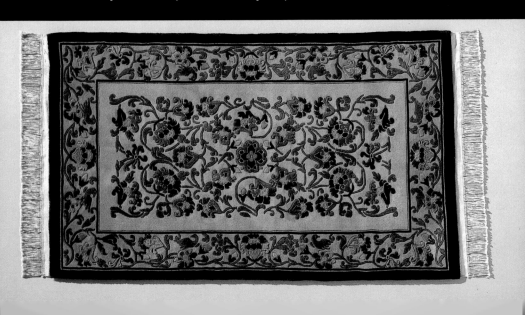

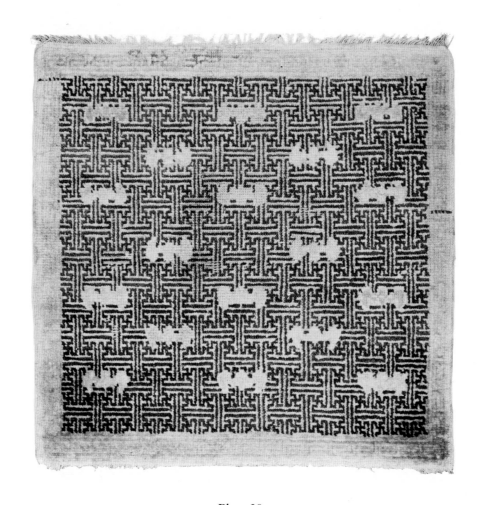

Plate 28

■ *Carpet woven in the Qing Dynasty. An all-over pattern of connected* wan *symbols and scattered bat motifs decorates this very early blue and gold carpet, possibly dating from the reign of Emperor Kangxi (1662–1722). Wool pile; cotton warp and weft; Senneh knots, c. 42 per square inch; 2' 6" x 2' 6¾" (0.76 m. x 0.78 m.). The Metropolitan Museum of Art, New York. Bequest of Ellis Gray Seymour, 1949.* ■

The Song Dynasty:
960–1279

The Song Dynasty, the weakest empire in the history of dynastic China, entirely altered many Tang practices, including that of placing carpets in every hall and of conducting important ceremonies upon them. The Tang taboo against leaving bare any part of a palace floor was no longer in effect. Carpet making is seldom mentioned in Song histories, but a changed attitude is readily apparent. Taizong, the second Song emperor (ruled 976–995), decreed that no money be appropriated for carpets in the newly constructed Longto Tianzhang Pavilion, in Kaifeng, Henan Province, the official building of a Grand Counselor. Also, by his decree, carpets already laid in the Hall of Prolonged Happiness were removed. The only carpet he allowed to remain was the refined carpet in the main ceremonial hall,[16] which covered the entire floor from wall to wall.

The attitude toward carpets was entirely different in the northern border districts, where animal husbandry was the mainstay of the economy. Rug making did not suffer there as it did in central and southern China. North China was still largely the home of nomads, who lived in tents and used carpets and rugs on their dirt floors, on the walls, and to cover the entrance to their tents (Plate 26).

Richer nomads spared no money in obtaining carpets to cover the floors of their principal rooms, and their search for exquisite quality and fine workmanship spurred the development of carpet making. Pile carpets appear to have attained a new level of excellence in this part of China, despite the lack of interest in carpets elsewhere.

Song poets wrote of the beauty and luxury of the carpets in the northern tents:

So white in color as a monk's collar guard
The cloth that he wore inside his robe,
So warm it keeps better than
the violet carpet
That was lying under the nomad's tent.

Su Dongpo (1037–1101)

Flickering I saw the scarlet flames
The stove was burning in the morn,
Rolled up in a nomad's rug,
Violet wools are soft on the bed.

Lu You (1125–1210)

In these poems the nomad tents are hospitable places, where visiting southerners were housed in quarters furnished with rich quality wool carpets dyed purple, a color normally reserved for the nobility because purple dyestuffs were so scarce. In the Tang and Song dynasties, purple was reserved by the emperor for his nobles. High officials were awarded gold medals attached to purple damask silk ribbons. Those next in the hierarchy were given silver medals with blue damask silk ribbons.

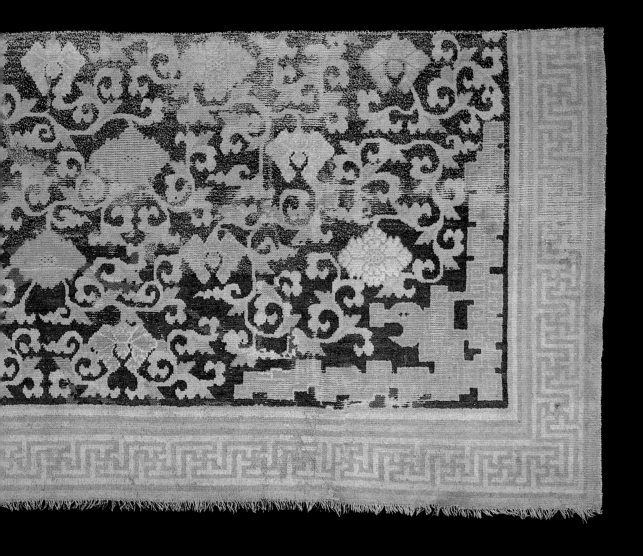

Plate 29

Fragment of a large carpet woven in the early nineteenth century. The inner corners of the central field show archaic dragons in guaizi *form (see Chapter 5). The border has faded. Wool pile; cotton warp and weft; Senneh knots; 4' x 10' 10" (1.20 m. x 3.33 m.). The Textile Museum, Washington, D.C.*

During this time a practical distinction between felt and pile carpets was made. They were used in different ways, felt mainly to cover the brick or earthen *kang,* pile mainly to cover the floor.

Carpets were occasionally seen in inland China, but only in the houses of nobles and the rich as a reflection of luxury, of a superior standard of living. Carpets also made valued gifts that influential families could exchange for official favors. It was traditional in that feudal society to procure all benefits by promising something of interest to officials in high places.

One story tells of a premier who was constructing a new house for his family, and whose subordinate, wise enough to want to please him, ordered magnificent pile carpets from Suzhou to fit the exact dimensions of the floor space throughout the house. The premier was so impressed by his subordinate's capability and experience that he awarded him repeated raises in grade. But in another story Qin Hui (1090–1155), the treacherous premier of the Southern Song Dynasty, was also building a new house, and his subordinate, Zheng Zhong, a regional inspector, did not fare so well when he attempted to please the premier by ordering a magnificent pile carpet from Sichuan to cover the floor of the premier's new house, called "Skyscraper Pavilion." Premier Qin, who at that time was involved in a political struggle for power, became angry that someone had made known the exact dimensions of his private house, thinking this would endanger his safety.

The Yuan Dynasty:
1279–1368

After ten years of fierce warfare with the Mongols, the Song empire fell. Thousands upon thousands of civilians were killed, urban and rural economies were disrupted, and social culture was strangled. The devastation was calamitous. The central power of China shifted to the Mongol Tartars, a strong, bellicose people who won control over a vast expanse of China mainly by their military success on horseback with bows and arrows. The progenitor of the Yuan Dynasty was Genghis Khan (1162–1227), the general who also swept over most of Central Asia and Eastern Europe. He was given the title Taizu ("Grandfather Emperor") posthumously, when his grandson Kublai Khan became the ruler of united China.

Strangely enough, during this period the art and skill of pile carpet making was not lost, but developed to a still higher level. The Mongols had lived in tents, and carpets were important to them. When the Mongol chiefs became the nobles in power they took a special census registering hundreds of thousands of households, including peoples living in Central Asia and the Indo-Chinese states, and among them found goldsmiths, silversmiths, tanners, stone engravers, jewelers, silk weavers, and pile carpet makers. They also recruited masters in all branches of handicrafts from the prisoners they had taken during the war of expansion, and these included many carpet makers.

Mastery in all the handicraft arts increased under the enforced Mongol rule of the Yuan Dynasty, and as carpet weavers improved their skill their art became more refined. They also benefited from contacts with Persian weavers who had been recruited into the masses of artisans —another instance of cultural exchange between East and·West. The Persian technique of close-piling joined the Chinese pattern designs, which used realistic objects rather than scattered geometric motifs.

When Marco Polo came to the imperial palace of Kublai Khan (1216–1294), in whose service he spent seventeen years, he exclaimed that the most exquisite carpets in the world were in the khan's possession.

Two different kinds of pile carpets were woven during the Yuan Dynasty, the patternless "clipped wool carpet" and the patterned "downy carpet" called both *ji* and *yangmaotan,* or sheep wool carpet. Both kinds were used as floor coverings. Felts were produced as well and, in addition to being used on the floor, were mold-pressed into skullcaps, boots for cold feet on icy ground, and covers for *kangs.* Commercially the felts were called *maozhan* (毛毡), which meant wool felt, a precise wording that distinguishes more clearly between carpets and felts than in the Song Dynasty. The word *tan* (毯), meaning blanket, appeared early in the fourth century, but by the Yuan

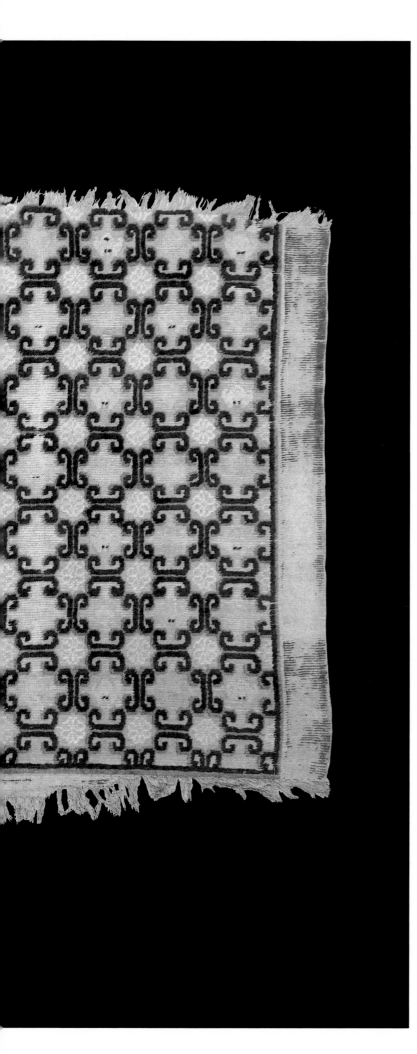

Plate 30

Carpet woven in the early nineteenth century for an imperial palace. It is unusual in that the warp lengths are shorter than the weft lengths. All the colors except indigo blue have faded. Stylized ruyi *clouds enclose either a bat or a floral rosette. Wool pile; cotton warp and weft; Senneh knots, 33 per square inch; 7' 8½" x 4' 3⅛" (2.35 m. x 1.305 m.). The Textile Museum, Washington, D.C.*

Dynasty it was used only for pile carpet in all parts of China.[17]

The average Han (native) Chinese family living in the Yellow River Valley under Mongol Tartar rule was miserable and poor and could not afford a covering on the floor. Yet there was always a sheet of wool felt on their earthen bed, which is still an indispensable piece of furniture in every northern Chinese home. *Kang* covers of wool pile were not widely used until the Qing Dynasty (1644–1911).

Carpets were woven in the government-owned carpet mills in Kambaliq (Beijing) and Holin, the northern capital of Yuan (now Horinger, Inner Mongolia). These carpets were of unprecedented quality and unequaled in the skill of their manufacture. According to one record[18] the equivalent of one *jin* (half a kilogram) of wool yarn was used to make one square *chi* (see Appendix II) of a sleeping carpet. Since one square *chi* was approximately equivalent to 1.2 square feet, this amount of wool roughly equals the weight used in a 90-line carpet today.

Skill in vegetable dyeing became mature in the Yuan Dynasty. Wool could be dyed in as complete a range of colors as vegetable dyeing permits. Carpets made in different localities could be distinguished by their most prominent color. One type was nicknamed Big Black after its dominant dark color, another Willow-Yellow because of the dominance of light yellow. In others persimmon-yellow, silver brown, and red predominated.

Natural-colored wool yarn was skillfully mingled with dyed yarns, and weavers began to distinguish between spring wool and autumn wool to get the best luster and resilience. They also learned how to mix coarse wool with fine to obtain different grades of yarn.

The Ming Dynasty:
1368–1644

Beginning in the 1340s, a series of native rebellions weakened the Mongol khans until in 1368 a peasant-general in command of a guerrilla army succeeded in expelling the foreign rulers. In the dynasty that he founded the artisans and workers were better off than in the Yuan Dynasty. No longer were they registered as prisoner-workers, nor did they work under surveillance. Their new status motivated an improvement in the handicraft arts. As a commodity economy formed, centers of handicrafts gradually developed. Family factories grew up here and there. As the deleterious effects of Mongol rule gradually lessened, skills and artistry surpassed those of the Tang and Song dynasties. Suzhou (Jiangsu Province) silk works, Songjiang (now Shanghai) cotton mills, Jingdezhen (Jiangxi Province) porcelain kilns, Zunhua (present-day eastern Hebei Province) iron foundries, and Wuhu (eastern Anhui Province) dyeing plants all grew considerably. Industries on a lesser scale were the carpet mills in what are now Ningxia Autonomous Region and Gansu Province. Carpet making during both the Ming and Qing dynasties flourished mainly in northwestern China.

Among the important customers of the northwestern carpet industry were the Lamaist temples and monasteries. Lamaism, a form of Buddhism that developed in Tibet, had prospered in China during the Yuan Dynasty. The famous Taersi monastery, or Stupa Temple, in Xi'ning was located in the heart of the Chinese carpet-making area. The Stupa Temple (Plate 32), a colony of Tibetan lamas situated 50 *li* (15 miles) southwest of Xi'ning, is named Gon Ben in the Tibetan language, which means "a hundred thousand Buddha images"; it is said to be the birthplace of Lozangia Ba, or Zongkaba (c. 1357–1419), founder of the Gelugpa Order, or Yellow Sect, of Tibetan Buddhism (Plate 31). His disciples built a stupa tower to store Buddha's bone relics, and gradually a large Lamaist temple grew up around the tower. In 1560 the Stupa Temple was completed as it stands today, a group of tall halls surrounding four big courtyards. Two of the halls are named Sockchin and Jao Ba, and other buildings include eighty mansions for the principal lamas, or Living Buddhas, and thousands of rooms for Lamaist monks. The main temple buildings are two large halls for worship with gilt copper tiles on the roofs. Other praying halls, mansions, and rooms are scattered about the valley, stretching to the foot of the mountain.

The area of Sockchin Hall is 21,300 square feet, the floor fully covered with prayer mats (Plate 33). One hundred and sixty-eight pillars support the heavy roof, all painted in colorful lacquer and wrapped with pillar carpets, and there are numerous curtained windows. Platforms on the floor are cov-

Plate 33 (opposite)
■ *Sockchin Hall, Taersi, Xi'ning,* ■
Qinghai. The entire floor (21,300
square feet; 1,981 square meters) as
well as the 168 pillars that fill the
room are covered with carpets: seat
mats, prayer mats, and pillar covers.
Sockchin Hall is regarded as the
principal place of exhibition for
carpets in northwestern China.

Plate 31
Statue of Zongkaba, founder of the
Gelugpa Order, or Yellow Sect, of
Tibetan Buddhism, in whose mem-
ory the Stupa Temple was built.
Taersi, Xi'ning, Qinghai.

Plate 32
■ *Taersi (Stupa Temple), Xi'ning,* ■
Qinghai.

ered with small seat mats of woven pile carpet.

The most elegant carpet is behind the statue of the Banchan Lama sitting on a Lotus Seat (see pages 93–94).[19] All of these carpets, rugs, and mats, together with the murals, sculptures, and embroidered satin and brocade, make the Stupa Temple a great artistic center, and it is regarded as the exhibition hall for carpets in the northwestern region. This temple was the most important patron of carpets from Ningxia and a model for other temples in Tibet and Mongolia for the methods of laying carpets on floors or hanging them on pillars and windows.

The various Ningxia carpets in the Stupa Temple were subsequently made for other temples and monasteries. The chief motifs, however, were not purely Buddhist: Ningxia carpets mingle Confucian, Taoist, and Buddhist motifs even though they were designed for Lamaist buyers. Such patterns depict *fu* (福), or "fortune," *lu* (禄), or "official grade and salary," *shou* (寿), or "long life," *xi* (喜), or "happiness," the harp, chessboard, books, and scrolls,

and the Eight Treasures of Taoism (see page 122). Even the carpets in the mansions of Living Buddhas were frequently decorated with such motifs as "rich and high-ranking," "longevity," "promotion in officialdom," "getting rich," "having more descendants," and "good fortune," even though the philosophy behind these motifs was contradictory to Buddhist asceticism. Several reasons account for this practice. Confucianism and Taoism were so ingrained in Chinese thought and ideology that no imagery could withstand their influence. The location of the Stupa Temple close to China's western border made possible the development of a hybrid mixture of religious concepts.

Chinese symbols and patterns based on Confucianism and Taoism seeped into the artifacts of the Tibetan tribes as well. Silk embroidery, porcelain, furniture, and carpets bearing inland Chinese symbols were accepted by the Tibetans indiscriminately. In Lhasa, the capital of Tibet, floor carpets in the Potala Palace and the Jablum Temple bear patterns showing Taoist spirits.

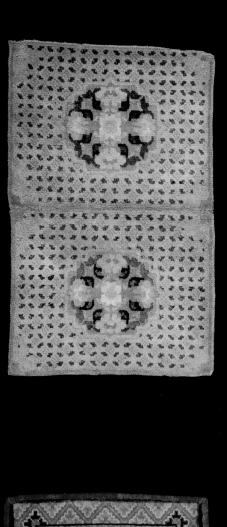

Plate 34 (left above)
This twentieth-century double car-pet was used as a prayer mat or seat mat in a Buddhist monastery. Wool pile; cotton warp and weft; Senneh knots, 42 per square inch; 1' 5¾" x 2' 3¾" (0.455 m. x 0.71 m.). The Textile Museum, Washington, D.C. Gift of Dr. William H. S. Stevens.

Plate 35 (left below)
These two squares of nineteenth- or twentieth-century pile carpeting were originally part of a long mat in a Buddhist prayer hall. Later they were converted into a saddle cover. Wool pile; cotton warp and weft; Senneh knots, 42 per square inch; each square 1' 7½" x 1' 7½" (0.50 m. x 0.50 m.). The Textile Museum, Washington, D.C.

Plate 36 (opposite left)
Probably dating from the eighteenth century, this carpet is of silk pile on a cotton warp and weft. It was de-signed as a seat cover for either a Buddhist monastery or a princely house. 2' 4⅞" x 2' 6¼" (0.74 m. x 0.755 m.). Royal Ontario Museum, Toronto, Canada.

Plate 37 (right above)
■ *Mat or rug woven in the nineteenth century for a Buddhist prayer hall. A fu-dog (see Chapter 2) forms the central motif. Wool pile; cotton warp and weft; Senneh knots, 27 per square inch; 2' 6½" x 4' 7½" (0.775 m. x 1.41 m.). The Textile Museum, Washington, D.C. Gift of William H. S. Stevens.* ■

Plate 38 (right below)
■ *Chair cover or seat mat woven in the mid-nineteenth century, perhaps as part of a long prayer-hall carpet. The motifs, which include fu-dogs, are woven in a simple antique color scheme of shades of blue on a gold ground. Wool pile; cotton warp and weft; Senneh knots, 30 per square inch; 2' 2⅜" x 2' 4⅜" (0.67 m. x 0.72 m.). The Textile Museum, Washington, D.C.* ■

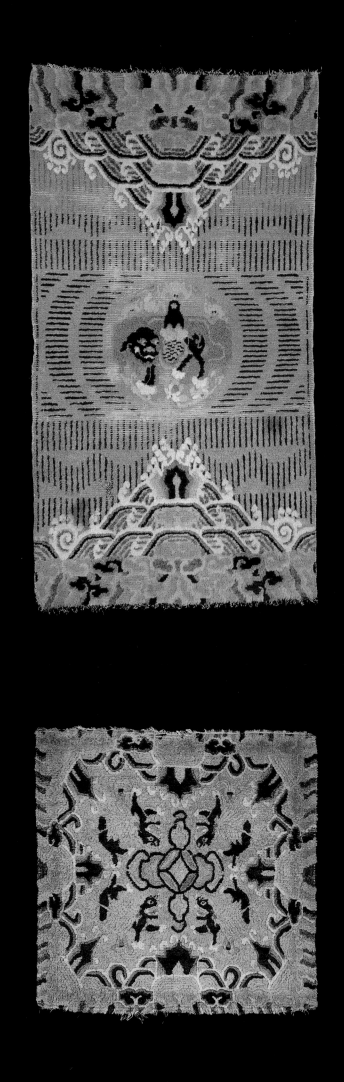

The dyes used during the Ming and
Qing dynasties by the northern peoples were principally a piercing blue
derived from indigo, a rich variety of
yellows from weld and other plant
sources, and a terra-cotta red from
madder roots, which sometimes with
age has faded into tan. Their color
combinations were simple. Some rugs
are woven in different shades of blue:
hence their name, Three Blues. All
these carpets were usually small and
rectangular, with clear, clean patterns
expressive in their simplicity (Plates
37, 38). Carpets ordered for the Lamaist temples and monasteries were magnificent in pattern, multicolored, and
woven in large sizes according to strict
standards of quality.

Plate 41
Carpet woven in the first half of the nineteenth century in Baotou, Inner Mongolia. The rug has a symmetrical, stylized floral pattern in three shades of blue, supplemented by an old gold or faded rust. Wool pile; cotton warp and weft; Senneh knots; 2' 1" x 3' 10⅞" (0.635 m. x 1.19 m.). Royal Ontario Museum, Toronto, Canada.

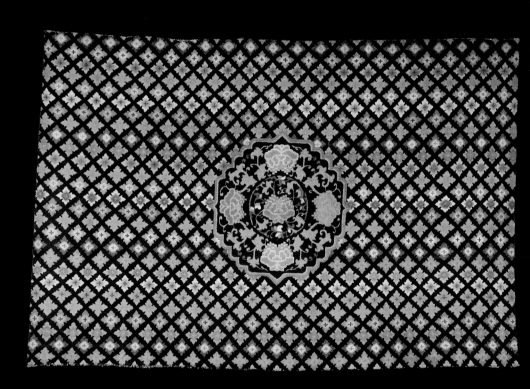

Plate 42
The geometrical all-over design of this carpet fragment, woven in the early twentieth century, suggests that it was made to order for a Western, perhaps American, customer. Wool pile; cotton warp and weft; Senneh knots, 42 per square inch; 5' 7⅜" x 8' 5⅛" (1.71 m. x 2.57 m.). The Textile Museum, Washington, D.C.

Plate 43

■ *Carpet woven in the mid-nineteenth century, probably in northwestern China. This example of Qing Dynasty carpet weaving is more elaborately decorated than the rug shown in Plate 1. The field between the corner ornaments and the medallion is filled in, and the borders are more complex, probably a result of the influence of Western taste. Wool pile; cotton warp and weft; Senneh knots, 42 per square inch; 6' 3⅝" x 9' 5" (1.92 m. x 2.87 m.).* ■
The Textile Museum, Washington, D.C.

The Qing Dynasty:
1644–1911

In 1644 Beijing, one capital of the Ming Dynasty, fell to the already victorious Manchu troops and the Qing Dynasty was established. (The first non-Han dynasty had been the Yuan, founded by the mighty Kublai Khan.) The Qing rulers were cautious about allotting power to other nationalities, particularly the Han Chinese, but gradually the two cultures became assimilated.

Like the Mongols, the Manchu Tartars were a warlike people who fought on horseback with bows and arrows. Constantly in the saddle, as are sheepherders on the Central Asian steppes today, they lavished attention upon their horses and military gear (Plate 46). Like the peoples of Mongolia, Tibet, and Xinjiang, they used carpets to cover the floors, walls, and doors of their tents. Small carpets, or blankets, were made to cover saddles of horses and camels (Plates 47–49). Before their conquest of China, the Manchus usually crafted their saddle covers

Plate 44
Painting in the Palace Museum, Beijing. Emperor Qianlong (1736–1795) is watching a wrestling match, and both his throne and the wrestlers are on carpets.

of felt, but later they had them hand-knotted in much the same manner as pile carpets—though the weave was sometimes more open, allowing more flexibility in the cloth; also, they were usually woven in two directions so that the pile always lay downward, making the blanket less irritating to the rider's thighs.

In many ways the Manchus continued their characteristic life after conquering the whole of China: they liked to camp in the wilderness when they went hunting, and every autumn the emperor held a drill at the imperial hunting enclosure, not solely for pleasure but as a military exercise as well. When camping in wilderness areas, carpets were a necessity, and the Tartars maintained this custom even in their houses in large cities north of the Yellow River. Owners of luxurious homes laid pile carpets between pieces of elegant wooden furniture. Beijing, the capital of the empire, was the center of wealth and

Plate 45

■ *Ancestor portrait of a military officer of the first rank and his wife. They wear fur-trimmed winter official costume embroidered with the three-clawed dragon. Under their chairs is an elegant carpet with a crane in the central medallion. Deer and cranes wander in the landscape beyond the pillars of the hall. Royal Ontario Museum, Toronto, Canada.* ■

Plate 46 (above)
Horses and riding gear, including saddle covers for hard wooden saddles, are still a necessity in northwestern China and Inner Mongolia, where sheepherders in the grasslands ride constantly. Here, modern Tadzik tribesmen engage in a sporting competition in the Pamir Mountains.

Plate 47 (right)
Saddle cover woven in the nineteenth century. The floral design in shades of blue on ivory recalls the designs on Chinese porcelains. Wool pile; cotton warp and weft; Senneh knots, 64 per square inch; 2' 1¼" x 4' 5⅛" (0.64 m. x 1.35 m.). The Textile Museum, Washington, D.C. Gift of Richard S. Woodbury, Charles Woodbury, and Mrs. Meylon H. Hepp.

Plate 48 (opposite left)
Saddle cover with an unusually graceful contour woven in the nineteenth century. Wool pile; cotton warp and weft; Senneh knots, 42 per square inch; 1' 10⅞" x 5' 3⅜" (0.58 m. x 1.61 m.). The Textile Museum, Washington, D.C. Gift of Richard S. Woodbury, Charles Woodbury, and Mrs. Meylon H. Hepp.

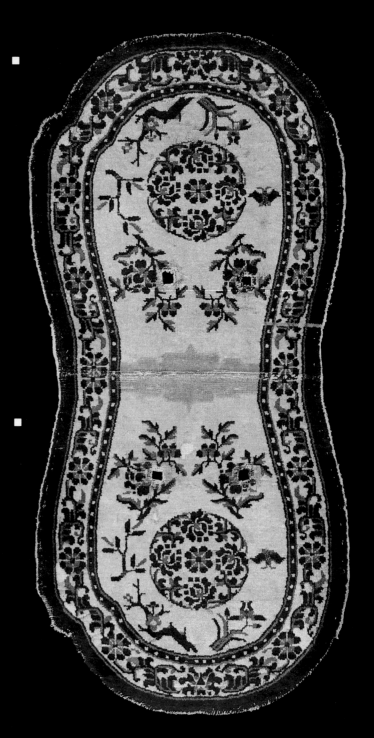

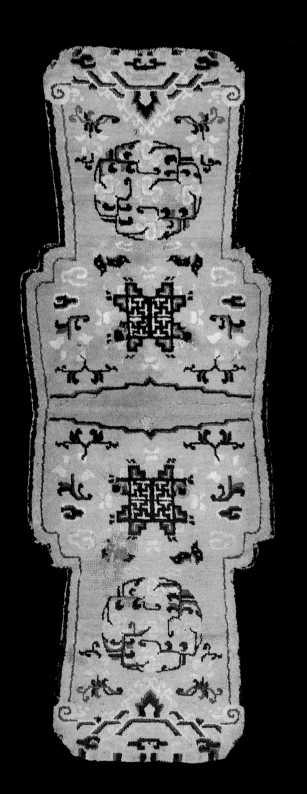

Plate 49 (above)
■ *Saddle cover woven in the nineteenth century.* ■
The endless-knot motif fills the field and wide
border. The holes were used when fitting the car-
pet over a saddle. Wool pile; cotton warp and
weft; Senneh knots, 62 per square inch; 1' 11" x
4' (0.585 m. x 1.22 m.). The Textile Museum,
Washington, D.C. Gift of Arthur D. Jenkins.

nobility, and, after the nomadic tent dwellers and the Buddhist temples, was the largest market for carpets. Nearly every North Chinese family had a *kang* with a pile carpet on it; the imperial palace had a *kang* in every bedroom, as we can see even now in the Palace Museum in Beijing. In South China, of course, there was no demand for warm, heavy floor coverings.

By the end of the sixty-year reign of Emperor Qianlong (1736–1795), the empire was prosperous and peaceful, except for border wars, and a boom in art and culture followed. Silk, porcelain, engraving on wood and stone, and carpet making reached great heights.

Qianlong was a fervent lover of carpets and ordered a great many of them. In the scene of one autumn drill on a painted scroll belonging to the Imperial Gallery (Palace Museum, Beijing), the emperor is seated on a dais under a canopy watching a group of wrestling warriors. Both the dais throne and the wrestlers are on carpets, the dais on a yellow carpet, the wrestlers on a larger carpet with floral designs. Judging from the size of the standing men, the larger carpet must be at least twelve by eighteen feet (Plate 44).

Both Qianlong and his grandfather Emperor Kangxi (ruled 1662–1722) were worshipers and patrons of Lamaist Buddhism, and in order to gain the support of the Mongolian and Tibetan minorities they had Lamaist temples built with government funds and endowed them with large annual appropriations for upkeep. In Inner Mongolia alone there were said to be over one thousand Lamaist monasteries, each headed by a principal lama having the title of Living Buddha.

On the route between the Yunghe Temple in Beijing and the famous Great Temple in Kulun (now Ulan Bator) there were 180 Lamaist temples, according to a rough count, and quantities of carpets covered every square inch of the important prayer halls as well as their columns and pillars, with prayer mats, seat cushions, and door curtains in addition.

The magnitude of the lamas' purchasing power was astonishing. Their demand for religious carpets inspired the workshops of Baotou, Yinchuan, Lanzhou, and Huangzhong, and carpet making became a prosperous industry in the northwestern districts. Moreover, Lamaist patronage enabled carpet making to survive as folk art in certain regions, such as Xinjiang, Ningxia, and Inner Mongolia, the upper reaches of the Yellow River, and Shanxi, Gansu, and Qinghai.

This booming market helped bring about advances in weaving skills and pattern design, and the northwestern school of carpet making was also enriched by an exchange of carpets of various sizes with the inhabitants of Mongolia, Tibet, and Xingjiang. Except for those from Xinjiang, present-day Chinese carpets are the descendants of this northwestern heritage.

Xinjiang carpets are different from the carpets made by the Han people of inland China, although the same figure-8, or Senneh, knot is generally used. The motifs and colors are similar to Central Asian carpets such as the Caucasian and Kazak types. In recent years this region, formerly called Chinese Turkestan by Westerners, has continued to develop its own characteristic styles and colors based on age-old traditions (Plates 50–53). In Hetian (Khotan), a Silk Route town in Xinjiang, midway between East and West, 3,000 carpets of various sizes were produced annually in the fifteenth century, and its artisans had developed excellent skills and artistic capabilities. Hetian carpets were sold to Afghanistan, India, and Europe, and many were shipped to the imperial court in Beijing. Among the treasures of the Palace Museum in Beijing is a group of elegant Hetian carpets purchased from Xinjiang by Qianlong especially to win the love of the legendary Fragrant Concubine (Concubine Rong), a Moslem and a Tadzik native. These rugs have exquisite natural motifs —stars shining on the clear blue background of an evening sky, seaside settings with creamy waves splashing against dark rocks, their spray of pearl droplets scattered all over.

The "Ningxia carpets" woven in Yinchuan (Ningxia Autonomous Region) and in the neighboring Alxazuoqi, a district in Inner Mongolia, were the best-known carpets of the Qing Dynasty. Sheep wool produced in Ningxia was graded Class A, for the Ningxia region benefited from irrigation, and the grass around the Yellow River bend was rich and abundant; this fertile environment fostered improvements in the quality of carpets produced there. Ningxia was also a trading center for northwestern China,

offering good means of transportation.

Ningxia carpet patterns combined designs traditional in carpet making with those used in carving wood and stone, weaving silk brocade, and making porcelain. Ningxia carpet making absorbed the lozenge forms and other geometric patterns from Hetian carpets (Plate 53); various auspicious motifs from enameled porcelain; and the Buddhist Eight Treasures symbols (see pages 123–24) from woven silk brocades and from the worshipers' sacrificial vessels in Lamaist temples. From the engraved bronze and silver vessels made in Mongolia and Tibet, the weavers took decorative patterns.

All these arts, in turn, resulted from the amalgamation of the arts of the Huihus,[20] the Huns, the western Qiangs, the Tibetans, and the Uighurs, and from cultures as far away as Persia, Arabia, and India. The considerable knowledge and skill acquired by these peoples and their burgeoning trade created a legacy in northwestern Chinese carpet making that modern Chinese weavers have inherited.

During the 1860s foreigners saw and began to appreciate the excellence of Chinese woolen carpets and to commission them for export to the British, European, and American markets, among others. There soon appeared a new trend in carpet design, brought about by the tastes of Western buyers. Noticeable changes were made in designs, patterns, and colors to appeal to this new market for carpets. Until that time most carpets had been produced by clans of herdsmen on the high plateaus, and elaborate patterns

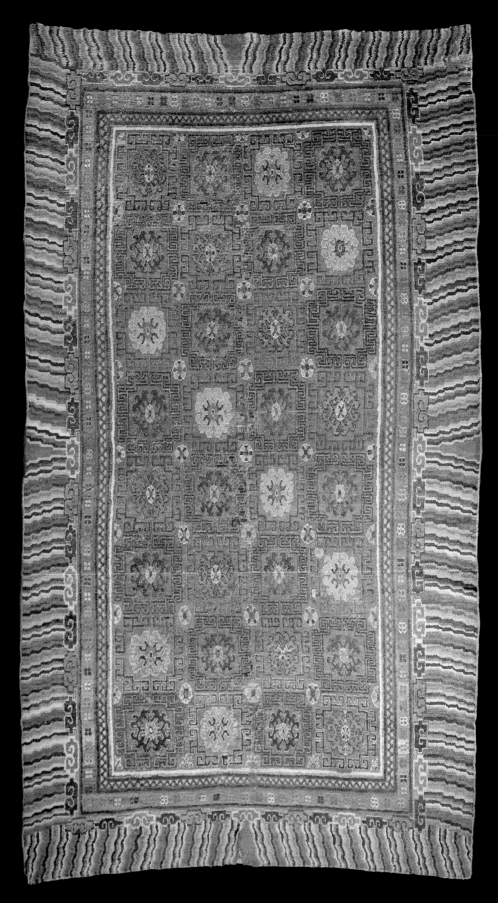

Plate 50

Xinjiang carpet woven in the nineteenth century. Within an elaborate frame of borders,
the outermost of which contains a stylized sea or wave pattern, is a field of fretted squares
containing stylized chrysanthemum motifs. Wool pile; cotton warp and weft; Senneh
knots, 32 per square inch; 6' 7⅛" x 12' 7¾" (2.01 m. x 3.70 m.). The Textile Museum,
Washington, D.C.

Plate 51
Carpet woven in 1981 in Urumqi, Xinjiang. Ancient and modern carpets from Xinjiang differ from inland Chinese carpets in color and design, reflecting the influence of Central Asian carpet weaving. Wool pile; cotton warp and weft; 6' x 9' (1.83 m. x 2.74 m.).

or complicated compositions were never included except where these were designed in workshops for royalty or wealthy individuals. But European fashion dictated that myriads of small details be added, that the solid Chinese patterns be shaken loose and the various elements scattered about the field (Plates 42, 43).

Some rugs had three or more borders, one inside the other. This kind of decoration for its own sake was an abrupt departure from the earlier Chinese concept of design and precise use of symbolism. To the Chinese it appeared strange, but they gave the foreign market what it preferred, while continuing to manufacture carpets in the traditional style, and these, too, were popular in foreign countries.

Beijing and Tianjin also developed into centers of carpet making during the Qing Dynasty, as the mastery of Ningxia weavers drifted eastward. The route of this eastward drift approximated the course of the Yellow River from Yinchuan in Ningxia to Baotou in Inner Mongolia; from there it went south to Shenmu in Shaanxi and east to Datong in Shansi, to Huhehot in Inner Mongolia, to Zhangjiakou in Hebei, and finally to Beijing.

Baotou was the key to this development; in the west lay Gansu and Ningxia, and a highway to the east connected Baotou to Beijing, easing communications overland and by boat. Baotou's location was therefore ideal for the burgeoning carpet industry.

When Zuo Zongtang (1812–1885), viceroy of Shaanxi and Gansu, led an army to suppress a rebellion in the northwest during the 1860s and 1870s, the cities and villages along his route were devastated by his brutal soldiers. The war of suppression lasted sixteen years, from 1862 to 1878, affecting the lives of millions.

Among the masses of refugees who fled to the east were two noted masters of carpet weaving, Xing (邢) and Tang (唐). They settled in Baotou and taught the workers in the carpet factories how to weave properly and dye better. After that the colors used in Baotou carpets increased in number, and simple patterns were supplemented by more complex designs. The name "Baotou carpet" gained in acceptance in northern Chinese markets. In style and quality they somewhat resembled Ningxia carpets, and the herdsmen and the monasteries in Mongolia began to buy large quantities of them. By 1920, one tenth of the population of Baotou, a small inland city of some 10,000 people, were engaged in carpet making. And to the present day, the masters Xing and Tang are acknowledged by the Baotou carpet craftsmen as the founders of their trade. The weavers and rug merchants worship them on Clear and Brightness Day (清明), usually April 5, traditionally a day of paying homage to the ancestors (see Appendix III).

Wealthy people and military officers increasingly demanded carpets that could be sent as gifts. Master Cui (崔师傅), a mural painter of temple walls, introduced into carpet design a pictorial or representational style. The motifs denoted auspiciousness and happiness and included Phoenix and a Rising Sun and Eight Immortals Congratulate a Birthday. Some of the picture patterns were historical, such as the Six Steeds of the Zhao Mausoleum (see page 108).

The emergence in the second half of the nineteenth century of pattern designers who painted carpet designs especially for weaving brought about a new system in the management of carpet making. For the first time a division of labor developed between the weavers and the designers, both learning from their own master-teachers by oral instruction and personal demonstration. This remains the traditional method of passing on the art and skill of carpet weaving.

Ningxia continued to be the center of carpet making in the middle reaches of the Yellow River, but Baotou carpets were produced in large quantities and compared well with the best carpets of Ningxia and Beijing-Tianjin.

In 1872, the eleventh year of the reign of Emperor Tongzi, son of the Empress Dowager Cixi (1835–1908), the Contract and Procurement Office of the Department of Imperial Internal Service appointed the monk Ordanima, a Tibetan Buddhist from Gansu Province, instructor in the carpet workshop organized by the department. The school was Baoguoszi (报国寺), a Buddhist monastery inside Zhangyimen (彰仪门), the southwest citygate of Beijing. Through this school in Beijing were formally introduced the Gansu-Ningxia weaving skills and designs; Beijing thus inherited the styles and folk quality that had flourished in the northwest provinces since the Ming Dynasty.

Treaties with Western powers forced the opening of trade ports in China, and the Manchu regime adopted a *laissez-faire* policy toward foreign trade, permitting the sale of Chinese carpets to be pushed abroad. In the 1880s, the Foreign Trade Agency (鲁麟洋行), a German firm in Tianjin, put Chinese carpets on the European market in quantity for the first time since the days of the Silk Route.

Russell & Company (旗昌洋行), an American firm, followed suit, and their small orders were the first recorded exports of Beijing carpets. Later, early in the twentieth century, many foreigners established agencies in Beijing and Tianjin for overseas distribution of Chinese carpets. Others organized and owned factories and workshops employing carpet designers and weavers to produce Chinese carpets and rugs for the European, British, and American markets.

Plate 52
Carpet woven during the first half of the nineteenth century in Hetian (Khotan), Xinjiang. Stylized chrysanthemums within fretted squares lie in orderly rows across the field. The border motif is yunshuitou ("cloud-water"). Unlike inland Chinese carpets, this one is knotted in Ghiordes, or horseshoe, knots (30 per square inch). Wool pile; cotton warp; wool weft; 4' x 7' 2" (1.219 m. x 2.184 m.). The Textile Museum, Washington, D.C. Gift of Jerome and Mary Jane Straka.

Plate 53

■ *Carpet woven early in the twentieth century, probably in* ■
Hetian (Khotan), Xinjiang. As is usual in Hetian designs of
this type, the pattern of the central medallion—in this
example the familiar vase and pomegranate motif—differs
from that of the other two. Wool pile; cotton warp and weft;
Senneh knots, 91 per square inch; 4' 1¼" x 6' 2" (1.25 m.
x 1.88 m.). The Textile Museum, Washington, D.C.
Gift of Dr. William H. S. Stevens.

Plate 54

■ *Weaver finishing a rug in Hetian (Khotan), Xinjiang, an* ■
important carpet-manufacturing center since ancient times.

Plate 55
■ *Self-Tone Embossed carpet woven in Shanghai in 1982. The sea and mountain design* ■
(shoushan fuhai) and a shou *symbol at center (see Chapter 2) have been sculptured and*
embossed on this cool, elegant gray rug. Wool pile; cotton warp and weft; Senneh knots,
90-line quality; 6′ x 9′ (1.83 m. x 2.74 m.).

The Modern Period:
1912 to the Present

The discovery of Chinese carpets by Western collectors in the late nineteenth century and early twentieth century resulted in a vigorous export trade and progress in several directions. Chinese and Western entrepreneurs experimented with and adopted machine-spun cotton yarns and chemical dyes and made other improvements in quality, while adhering to the traditional hand-knotting technique. Most early modernization took place in the eastern regions, around Tianjin and Beijing, where owners and managers were able to order materials from overseas suppliers and to collect them at nearby ports of entry; producers in the northwest tended to retain the old methods and materials.

When chemical dyes were adopted, a greater variety of colors and color combinations could be achieved, and a "custom" service was established, with eastern workshops filling overseas orders according to each buyer's request. Chemical washing was introduced during this period and it gained for Chinese carpets increased acceptance abroad. In Tianjin experiments were undertaken to conceal the weft on the backs of carpets. This resulted in the "closed-back" hand-knotting technique described in Chapter 3.

By the 1930s machine-spun yarns were used almost everywhere for both warps and wefts and, occasionally, for the wool pile. At about the same time,

craftsmen in Tianjin invented the techniques of incising, carving, and embossing that are unique to Chinese carpets, distinguishing them to this day from most other hand-knotted carpets in the world.

The symbols that had been important in Chinese folklore, tradition, philosophy, and religion for thousands of years remained the motifs used in carpet design, but designers began to assemble them in new ways that often broke the constraints of tradition, and they also created new designs to satisfy Western taste. In addition, Western importers sent their own designs and colors for carpets to be produced for their markets. They bought many carpets during the 1920s and 1930s, introducing Art Deco and French Aubusson (now called Esthetic) designs, which became extremely popular (Plate 122). Many of these carpets and rugs are still in use and remain in good condition.

In 1937, with the occupation of eastern China by Japan, the export of carpets to the West declined. By 1941 shipments had ceased completely and the freeze remained in effect until 1946. Efforts were made to start trade up again in the late 1940s but they met with little success because of an unsettled business climate, uncontrolled inflation, and widespread corruption and civil war in China. In 1949 the People's Republic of China was established and shortly afterward the government recruited experienced carpet makers who reshaped the industry in its present form.

In recent years there has been a revival of interest in Chinese carpets old and new. Collectors, interior designers, and the general public have come to appreciate these fine floor coverings of excellent value, quality, and durability, which can be adapted to meet individual requirements, and achieve a timeless beauty in richness of color and harmony of design.

---

[1] The Qiangs have been a minority tribe in China since ancient times. Their most important settlement today is in north Sichuan Province.

[2] L. Carrington Goodrich, *A Short History of the Chinese People*, 3d ed., New York, 1959, p. 19.

[3] *Zhouli (The Rituals of Zhou,* 周礼), *Tianguan* chapter.

[4] One of the Five Classics, *Shangshu (Documents from High Authority)* is a collection of official documents dating from the Shang and Zhou dynasties.

[5] This figure, much larger than the one usually cited, is a Chinese statistic that takes into account the fact that the Wall is sometimes a double rampart. Zigging and zagging, it crosses five provinces, from Shanhaiguan ("Pass of Mountain and Sea") in Hebei to Jiayuguan ("Pass of Auspicious Valley") in Gansu.

[6] Liu Bang was given the title Gaozu ("High Progenitor") posthumously.

[7] A *kang* is a raised platform used as a bed in North Chinese homes. Usually of earthen or brick construction, it is hollow inside, and in the winter it is heated. Warmth from a fire outside the bedroom (often the kitchen fire) flows through a narrow tunnel into the chamber beneath the bed. A pile carpet is laid on top of the *kang* to serve as a mattress.

[8] *History of the Han Dynasty*, vol. 23.

[9] From the book *Yiyuan*. The governor was magistrate of Taiyuan, Shanxi Province.

[10] In the Western world these are called Ghiordes knots or Turkish knots.

[11] After a row of knots has been tied, this tool is used to pound the knots down tightly against the weft. Today weft dabbers are made of iron and are quite heavy (Plate 95).

[12] The Nestorian priest Rabban came to the Tang capital in 635.

[13] The first Moslems came to China in 632.

[14] *Imperial Decrees and Edicts of the Tang Dynasty*, vol. 103. Nestorians and Zoroastrians were also prosecuted: "They shall be compelled to return to secular life lest they continue to contaminate the customs of China."

[15] An important staging center on the Silk Route in northwestern China. Here worshipers created hundreds of cave temples in which they erected statues of the Buddha and his disciples and also painted murals. These caves served traveling Buddhists as places of worship and study.

[16] *Historical Records of the Song Dynasty*, "Food and Other Commodities" chapter.

[17] *Ditan* is the word used for floor covering in China today.

[18] *Historical Records of the Yuan Dynasty*, "Manufactured Articles" chapter.

[19] The Dalai Lama and the Banchan Lama were the supreme power holders in Tibet under the Qing Dynasty (1644–1911). As living reincarnations of the Buddha, both took great interest in the Stupa Temple in Xi'ning. By 1800 the number of monks in the temple had increased to about 3,000 and learned monks of the first degree, or Living Buddhas, were in the hundreds.

[20] The Huihus were a tribe in the border districts of Xinjiang and Gansu. Their descendants still live there as one of China's thirteen minority nationalities residing in those areas.

2. SYMBOLS AND SYMBOLISM

One hundred forms of the shou *character symbol, expressing a wish for the gift of longevity*

A culture is inseparable from its symbols. In our discussion of Chinese symbols certain ideas will appear again and again—ideas of hope and happiness, wishes for prosperity and long life. These ideas suggest a generally optimistic culture.

The definition of a symbol is only an outline of its meaning. Symbols are used because they are suggestive and it is paradoxical to attempt to sum up the meaning of a symbol in a few words. The number of Chinese symbols reflects a basic philosophical tradition, that the "best statement is one that does not fall into the net of words."[1] For words are limiting; what is not said can be as expressive as what is said. In explaining the meaning of a work of art, the ideas are limited by the very words of description. The significance of art goes beyond words; to experience it involves all the senses.

When we look at a rug and explain its patterns and motifs, we are to some degree limiting the rug's meaning. The explanation translates the rug's symbols into our own words and thereby brings up our own ideas. The problem is similar to that of translating literature, especially poetry, from one language to another, for the original suggestiveness may lose much of its richness through translation. Explanations provide a key to understanding the language of Chinese carpet design, but additional knowledge of Chinese culture will unlock more doors and progressively enrich the experience.

For a Chinese rug is more than an ornamental covering for a wall or floor, it is a kind of adventure. The rich, complex, and ancient culture of China and its people partially reveals itself to us through a variety of designs and patterns that are actually traditional Chinese symbols. These symbols form a language that tells us about the past and present, about the personalities, emotions, ideas, and beliefs of a people who for thousands of years have expressed their prayers, fears, hopes, and joys in the shape of flowers and creatures, and in symbols of living things and forces of nature.

Each peony, dragon, wave, and scroll in a rug constitutes part of a symbolic language also used in paintings, ceramics, bronzes, tapestries, clothing, architecture, furniture, and utensils, telling something of what the Chinese have thought and felt during the more than 3,000 years of life and death and recorded history, across the vast reaches of their country.

Such are the thoughts represented by the symbolism in a Chinese rug. It may be that a poem or a story is spread out before us, or a beautiful, skillfully woven, eminently practical adventure, told in the symbols of a language anyone can understand because we all share the experience of our common humanity.

Plate 56

■ *Carpet woven in Shanghai in 1976. The field features bamboo and plum blossom motifs,* ■
symbolizing success and the Five Blessings. The border contains auspicious emblems:
peonies, butterflies, and another scattering of plum blossoms. Wool pile; cotton warp and
weft; Senneh knots, 90-line quality; 6' x 9' (1.83 m. x 2.74 m.).

Hundreds of symbols and designs representing feelings, ideas, historical events, legends, hopes, fears, joys, and sorrows have been woven into Chinese rugs. The rugs may be beautiful and please our sense of color and design, but through symbols they also express ideas that have connections with many aspects of Chinese culture—history, philosophy, religious beliefs, and customs of daily life. Virtually all of these symbols are auspicious or felicitous in meaning. Some of the motifs discussed in this chapter may not be seen in carpets produced today; they are included because they help in dating ancient pieces and in interpreting their symbolism correctly.

The symbols in Chinese rugs, as in all Chinese art, in addition to reflecting more general aspects also express specific ideas from the three philosophical and religious influences that prevailed for so long in China. Some of these symbols are complex; often they are obscure; sometimes they are inseparable from the Chinese language. Historically, Chinese art was the domain of scholars, and many works of art speak to the intellect as well as the senses. As we learn about these symbols we learn about the ideology of some of the Chinese people. As we learn more in this respect, our understanding of these symbols continually broadens.

A Chinese carpet can be an intellectual experience as well as an aesthetic one. The following discussion of symbols should help the reader understand Chinese rugs and carpets on this intellectual level and may strengthen his emotional response to the rugs as his appreciation grows for the Chinese culture, its history, and its people.

When a Westerner thinks of Chinese paintings, he probably remembers its lovely birds and the many scenes of landscapes and mountains. The Chinese people have a deep love for their country and its resources, and Chinese artists have always had a profound affinity for the natural world. Forms from nature provide dominant motifs in Chinese rugs and carpets, motifs that may be beautiful but are figurative as well, for each flower, tree, bird, or animal has its specific meaning.

The strong bond between the Chinese people and nature is reflected in Taoist and Buddhist imagery. These philosophies and religions will be discussed in further detail, but for now, it is important to understand that they share an aspiration toward harmony with nature. While Judaism and Christianity consider man to be God's greatest accomplishment, the Chinese philosophies and old religions view man as only one element in the larger scheme of nature.

In the West, Michelangelo carved his *David* as a tribute to man, and hence to God. Through the ages, Chinese artists believed that harmony with nature led to spiritual satisfaction, and they focused much of their time and talent on tributes not to man, but to nature's many living forms. These include flowers, trees, birds, and animals, and since these are among the more recognizable symbols in Chinese rugs, we will begin our adventure with them.

The relationship between language and many of these symbols is crucial, however, and our discussion of the individual symbols must start with a brief explanation of homophones, words that sound alike but have different meanings. In English they often cause confusion in spelling: piece and peace; vain, vane, and vein. They are at the heart of much wordplay in speech and literature, especially in the form commonly known as puns. We will discover many Chinese symbols that derive their meaning from homophones. To take one common example —the bat: homophonic are the Chinese words for bat, *bianfu* (蝙蝠), and for happiness, *fu* (福), which also means blessing or prosperity. The bat thereby takes on very favorable emblematic connotations.

Plants

PEONY. The beautiful, silky petaled peony is an important theme in Chinese literature and watercolor painting.

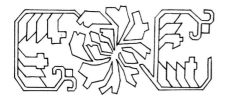

Archaic-style peony border

The flower thrives best in northern China, especially in Henan Province, whose emblem it is. The Chinese word for peony is *mudan*, a combination of "male" (*mu*) and "vermillion" (*dan*). These words suggest the large, showy, and variegated qualities of peony blossoms. The Chinese hail the peony as King of the Flowers, and consider it a symbol of unparalleled beauty, love, and affection. It is also considered the flower of riches and honor. Because the peony blooms in the spring it is an emblem of that season (Plate 84).

Archaic-style peony

LOTUS. The lotus is the Flower of Summer and, by extension, of happiness and fruition in maturity. It has significance in many other cultures: in ancient Egypt it became a symbol for the Nile itself, the giver of life, because the lotus grew as a water lily on the Nile; in Indian mythology it draws special importance from its close link with Buddhism.

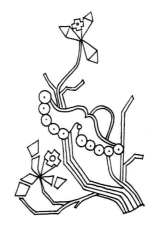

Archaic-style lotus blossom

China had an ancient regard for the lotus blossom, but its symbolic value became enhanced after the Buddhist faith was introduced. The lotus grows in swamps and marshes, stemming from mud but not defiled. This plant thus signifies a person morally clean and upright, untainted by the evil that surrounds him. A Buddhist paradise is strewn with lotus blossoms, symbols of purity and perfection. The lotus often serves as the seat of Buddha in

painting and sculpture. This Lotus Seat, or Sumeru Seat, is actually a round platform surrounded with up-turned lotus petals. One of the most important Buddhist texts is called the Lotus Sutra.[2] In Buddhist theology, the man who followed the ways of the Buddha would emerge as the lotus, pure and perfect (Plate 57).

The lotus has two names in Chinese, *he* (荷), a homonym for "peace and harmony," and *lian* (莲), meaning repeated good fortune. The amply filled seedpod of the lotus also symbolizes fertility or progeny.

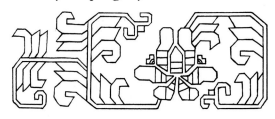

Archaic-style lotus-blossom border

Plate 58 (above)

■ *Carpet woven in Shanghai in 1978. Archaic dragons coil among lotus and shou motifs.* ■
Wool pile; cotton warp and weft; Senneh knots, 90-line quality; diam. 5' (1.54 m.).

Plate 57 (opposite)

This carpet made in the early nineteenth century in Xinjiang was probably used as a seat
mat by a Living Buddha. The lotus is a prominent motif in carpets woven for monasteries,
for it symbolizes purity to the Buddhist faithful. Here, lotus blossoms fill both the border
and the field of the rug. Silk pile; cotton warp and weft; Senneh knots, 100 per square
■ *inch; 3' 4¼" x 3' 5¼" (1.025 m. x 1.05 m.). The Textile Museum, Washington, D.C.* ■

CHRYSANTHEMUM. Chrysanthemums bloom in the autumn and are a Chinese symbol for that season. As a flower in the waning months of the year, the chrysanthemum is often associated with long life and the quiet days of retirement. In the past this flower was a favorite of scholarly officials, who sometimes devoted their last years to their gardens. Taoists believed that an infusion of dried chrysanthemum petals in wine engendered longevity.

Archaic-style chrysanthemum

Archaic-style plum blossom

PLUM BLOSSOM. The plum tree characteristically lives for many years. In Zhejiang Province there is a plum tree that supposedly was planted during the Sui Dynasty (589–618). Long life and blossoms that appear in the cold of winter make the plum a suitable symbol of the person who withstands difficulties. It also symbolizes winter itself, especially in combination with flowers symbolizing the other seasons (Plate 84).

In carpet patterns a flower having five petals signifies a plum. The five petals connote a host of lucky or favorable "fives," notably the Five Blessings, a collective term for the highest desires in life, dating back to *Shangshu,* one of the Classics: long life, wealth, health and peace, love of virtue, and a natural death (Plate 56).

ENSEMBLE OF FOUR FLOWERS. The summer's lotus and the spring-blooming peony often appear with autumn's chrysanthemum and the plum blossom of winter, this ensemble representing the four seasons. The cycles of nature are of crucial importance to cultures having strong links with the soil, and the universal harmony between man and nature is exemplified by the endless cycle of the seasons (see Appendix III). The ensemble of four flowers is common in Chinese carpets.

PEACH. Chinese mythology considers the Heavenly Peach Garden to be the source of immortality, because that fruit brings immortality to whoever eats it; the god of longevity is often pictured holding a peach. The symbolism of the peach is closely associated with the Taoists, who called it the "fairy fruit" because of its magical properties. The Taoists had a consuming interest in finding an elixir of immortality, and the fruit and bark of the peach tree were primary substances of their "elixir vitae." The peach in various forms, including peach stones, objects made of peach tree wood, and wreaths of peach blossoms, were used to dispel evil spirits.³ Since marriages were traditionally performed in the spring, the spring-blooming peach sometimes represents a young bride.⁴

POMEGRANATE. The pomegranate was brought to China from Central Asia before 100 B.C. It is a natural symbol of hope for numerous offspring, for it displays a multitude of seeds when it bursts open. The pomegranate is often depicted this way in traditional carpet designs, half open with some of its seeds exposed. This pattern is named *Liukai Baizi* ("one hundred seeds at the gap of a pomegranate"). This emblem of fertility and posterity is often found in Xinjiang carpets and also in many carpets made before 1911 in the northwest (Plates 2, 53).

BUDDHA'S HAND. As this fruit grows, it extends into a configuration resembling a human hand: thus its name, *foshou,* or Buddha's hand. It is said to symbolize wealth and honor (Plate 62).

This fruit has the scientific name of *citrus medica.* Although the pulp is inedible, its peel may be candied and it is served as dessert in homes in central China. It is often placed in a bowl so that its strong fragrance will scent the room.

PLANT OF IMMORTALITY (LINGZHI). This plant is a species of fungus that usually grows at the roots

of trees. In an old Chinese dictionary it is described as "the divine plant," and legend says that it brought immortality to those who ate it. Only the deer and phoenix could find the fungus, which was thought to grow high in the mountains and on the Taoists' Three Islands of the Immortals. The *lingzhi* motif is frequently grouped with the crane, pine, peach, and tortoise, and other symbols of longevity.

An ancient scepter, or *ruyi* (如意), said to take its form from the plant, is a symbol of unlimited power. Its name literally means "as you wish it," phrase that came to mean the fungus as well.

Plate 59
■ *Ancient ceramic decoration on a wall of the Palace Museum, Beijing,* ■
showing mandarin ducks playing under lotus leaves.

Plate 60 (opposite)
■ *Detail of frontispiece. Cranes, bats, clouds, and the ancient trident called* ■
ji, emblematic of "good omen," stand out boldly against a field of blue.
The Textile Museum, Washington, D.C.

BAMBOO. Bamboo is a favorite motif in Chinese art. One of the more distinguished painters of bamboo was Wu Chen (1280–1354), a scholar of the Yuan Dynasty, who inscribed the following poem in one of his paintings:[5]

Tender are the flowers of spring.
Willows swaying softly in the wind;
But these gentlemen alone will remain
The friends of winter's cold.

The "gentlemen" of the inscription are bamboo plants, hardy and enduring. Scholars, often persecuted for their intellectual independence, saw the bamboo as symbolic of their own ideals and their role in society, for with its hollow core and pliant strength the bamboo can be bent but not easily broken.

The hardy bamboo is often depicted with other winter-sustaining emblems, such as pine and plum trees. The combination, sometimes called the "three friends," symbolizes mental strength that can withstand reverses. The bamboo also represents auspiciousness— good luck—for the Chinese word for "wish" (*zhu*) sounds the same as the name for bamboo (*zhu*), another homophonic symbol found in carpet designs (Plate 56).

Birds and Animals

The world of animals and birds occupies a wide field in Chinese symbolism, and indeed many cultures find meaning, pleasure, and magical properties in them. They can represent many things: some are stronger than man, some live longer and are more prolific, and some are necessary to agriculture. The Chinese belief in nature's universal harmony demands that men share a balanced existence with the animals, whose symbols are another rich source of motifs in Chinese rugs.

CRANE. The species of crane called *grus japonesis* has a scarlet scalp. In the Manchu court, a civil official of the first degree wore on his official coat a square badge embroidered with a white crane, and on top of his official cap a red coral button. The *grus japonesis* thus became an emblem of a first-degree official (Plate 78). The crane appears frequently in Chinese art, and Chinese legend endows it with many mythical attributes. The crane is reputed to be the patriarch of the feathered tribe, and a favorite companion and vehicle for immortals and fairies. A common emblem for longevity, it is often depicted in or under a pine tree, another symbol of age; together these symbols connote the promise of prolonging life indefinitely.

CHINESE BULBUL. This bird is identified by its white head. The bulbul is a symbol of conjugal fidelity; a pair of bulbuls, often depicted, represents the promise of living to a ripe old age in conjugal bliss.

MAGPIE. The magpie is a common bird in China and regarded as a good omen. The Chinese name for this bird, *xique* (喜 鹊), means "bird of joy." It is traditionally believed that a family will have good luck if a magpie builds its nest near their home. The chattering of magpies before a house means that guests will arrive in the near future.

The Chinese have a saying, "The magpie sends in a message of safety." If a man is debating with himself about the success of some plan and he

Plate 61

■ *Carpet made in Shanghai in 1980. There are two bats with a* shou *symbol and meander design in each corner of the central field. A group of five bats (wufu) encircle the central medallion. The border design is adapted from motifs on Shang Dynasty bronzes. Wool pile; cotton warp and weft; Senneh knots, 90-line quality; 6' x 9' (1.83 m x 2.74 m.)* ■

Plate 62
A pair of fish means "wedded bliss." On this carpet sample they swim beside peach and buddha's-hand motifs, which are emblematic of long life and honor.

Plate 63
Stone lion guarding a gate in the Forbidden City, Beijing.

suddenly hears the magpie's joyous voice, he will accept the bird's song as encouragement.

PARADISE FLYCATCHER. The paradise flycatcher is another example of homophonic symbolism. The flycatcher's name in Chinese is *shoudainiao* (绶带鸟), "ribbon bird." *Shou* sounds like the word for longevity, so the bird is a symbol for long life.

MANDARIN DUCK. This small waterfowl was called the mandarin duck by Westerners in China because its bright, colorful plumage resembled the dress of the mandarins (officials) in imperial China (Plate 59).

These beautiful ducks display a notable attachment for their mates and are said to pine away and die if they become separated. Such behavior has made the mandarin duck an emblem of conjugal fidelity.

BAT. A common motif in Chinese carpets, the bat was mentioned earlier in the definition of homophones (see page 92). It is not regarded with aversion as in the West. The animal is often seen in combination with other figures to form elaborate messages.

For decorative purposes the bat often has so ornate a form that it resembles a butterfly. A group of five bats, *wufu* (五福), represents the Five Blessings: long life, wealth, health and peace, love of virtue, and a natural death (Plate 61).

■ *Bats in many different forms may be seen on Chinese carpets and furniture. When bats encircle the Chinese character called* shou *("longevity")—forming the image in the center of the drawing—the message is "long life and happiness together"* ■

DEER. Deer are believed to live very long and they became another symbol for longevity. The ancients believed the deer to be the only living animal having the wisdom or ability to find the *lingzhi*, the sacred fungus of immortality. The Chinese name for white-spotted deer, *lu* (鹿), is similar in pronunciation to the word for official wages, and this deer is symbolic of money in this form.

LION. Most Westerners have seen photographs of stone lions that guard the gates of important buildings in China (Plate 63). These lions were originally set in front of palaces, temples, monasteries, and mausoleums to scare off demons. Although the lion is not native to China, these representations became common there when Buddhist tradition introduced the lion as the defender of law and protector of sacred buildings. To the Chinese the lion is also a symbol of valor and energy.

The traditional place of lions in front of buildings is with the male on the east side of the gate (important buildings are usually oriented with the gate facing south), its right front paw grasping an engraved ball; on the west side is the lioness, its left paw caressing a playful cub.

This lion is magnified, with an enlarged head, inordinately thick mane, and muscular breast, intended as a playfully grotesque rather than a realistic representation.

FISH. The fish is a symbol having many meanings in Chinese culture. The word for fish is *yu* (鱼), and in another example of homophony, the Chinese word for superfluity makes the fish symbolize abundance or wealth— a symbolism made stronger by the fact that fish are so plentiful in Chinese waters.

A pair of fish is a common betrothal gift to the family of a bride-to-be as a good-luck symbol, a wish that the marital union may be happy (Plate 62). The symbol is also found in a Buddhist legend that lists the fish among the auspicious charms on the footprints of Buddha, the purpose of these charms being to avert evil.

CARP. This fish is called *li* (鲤) in China, and it is symbolic of profit or benefit because these words sound alike.

Perseverance is another emblematic meaning of the carp because it wages a struggle against the river currents. They are sometimes called the sturgeon of the Yellow River; legends say that carp ascended the river annually in the third moon of the year. The carp's rough scales and whiskers were thought to resemble a dragon's and the fish that swam through the rapids at Longmen ("Dragon Gate") are said to be transformed into dragons. Thus, the carp symbolized eminence or a scholar who has "passed every hurdle."

HORSE. The horse is a motif sometimes used on Chinese rugs (Plate 64). This animal has been significant in Chinese history: it caused the life of the northern tribes, notably the Mongols, to change from pastoral to nomadic, and with their superior mobility they invaded China repeatedly, even overthrowing ruling dynasties.

The Chinese emperors early recognized the advantages of a cavalry and developed the horse and chariot into an effective mobile army during the Shang Dynasty. The Han emperor Wudi took a special interest in acquiring fine horses, sending envoys to the king of Ferghana, in Central Asia, to exchange silk for a particular breed of horse known for its strength and speed. The emperor called it the Heavenly Horse.

Under military rulers from the Han to the Mongol Yuan dynasties and down through the Qing, whose rulers had won their empire on horseback, horses were popular subjects in art, especially in sculpture. Figures of pow-

Plate 64

Carpet made in Tianjin in 1979. The central medallion is a motif copied from an ancient bronze excavated in 1969 in Gansu Province. To express the swiftness of the horse, one hoof is shown poised on a flying swallow. Wool pile; cotton warp and weft; Senneh knots, 90-line quality; 6' x 9' (1.83 m. x 2.74 m.).

Plate 65

■ *Carpet woven in Shanghai in 1976. A fu-dog looks out playfully from the center of the field, and ancient coins appear in the outer border in groups of two and three. The large number of emblems and the elaborate border treatment make this an unusual piece. Wool pile; cotton warp and weft; Senneh knots, 90-line quality; 6' x 9' (1.83 m. x 2.74 m.).* ■

erful horses were placed outside imperial tombs, on guard against demons.

Emperor Taizong of the Tang Dynasty (ruled 626–649) so loved the horses he had ridden on the battlefields during his victorious campaigns to unify China that his mausoleum at Xi'an was decorated along the entrance with six stone reliefs that commemorate his devotion, each relief representing one of his favorite horses. Together they were called the Six Steeds of the Zhao Mausoleum (Plate 10).[6] The horse became a symbol of wealth and prestige through its association with the ruling emperors.

FU-*DOG*. The *fu*-dog, or pekingese, is popularly believed to have been sent to China from Anatolia as a present to an emperor in the seventh century A.D. The breed soon made popular pets in aristocratic families. The playful toy dog sometimes appears as a carpet motif, usually with an exaggeratedly large head and ruff, for, like the lion, it symbolizes strength and courage (Plate 65).

DRAGON. Perhaps no animal is seen more frequently in Chinese painting and sculpture, or pottery, fabric, and rug design than the dragon. The Eastern dragon is not the gruesome monster of medieval imagination and folktales in the West, but a genius of strength and goodness. The word for dragon, *long* (龙) remains so familiar and beloved that even today it plays an important part in the Chinese language. The only word in China for a faucet is "dragon's head," derived from the dragon's close association with bodies of water. On festival days young people compete with one another in "dragon boats"; the rural adage "to snatch food from the dragon's mouth" encourages people to hasten the cutting and transporting of wheat before a sudden storm can ruin the harvest, the adage coming from the dragon's reputed control of the climate.

One of the dragon's most important aspects is its power to bring clouds and rain. The agrarian cultures understood that drought and flooding controlled their very existence, and in ancient times four dragon kings who ruled the seas were worshiped in China, especially at harvest time.

The dragon originated as the totem of an early Chinese clan, the Xia, and throughout the ages the dragon underwent many changes. On the bronze vessels of the Zhou Dynasty dragons are grotesque monsters with long horns, curved body, and a fish-like tail. From inscriptions on Zhou dragons comes the name *kui* (夔), and all dragons of grotesque appearance are now called *kuilong*, also known as the archaic dragon. Despite his visage, the *kuilong* is a beneficent creature, his many powers including a restraining influence over the sin of greed. He is said to have nine sons, and they too occasionally appear on carpets.

The dragon's form and reputation continued to flourish in the Han Dynasty and it assumed an ensemble of features adopted from many animals. It grew in influence until it supposedly had almost all climatic changes under its power, including flood and drought, rain and clouds, and thunder and lightning: "He unfolds himself in the storm clouds; he washes his mane in the blackness of the seething whirlpools. His claws are in the fork of the lightning, his scales begin to glisten in the bark of rain-swept pine trees. He slowly rouses himself into activity and quickens a new Spring."[7] The creature became associated with the Han Dynasty when Emperor Gaozu established the divinity of kings in 206 B.C. and from then on the dragon was the emblem of imperial power. The throne, robes, and all household articles of the emperor carried the dragon symbol.

Imperial use of the dragon during the Ming Dynasty developed further. It was declared that the five-clawed dragon could only be used by the emperor and his son, or by princes of the

Plate 66
Carpet woven early in the nineteenth century. Archaic dragons, each guarding a jewel, are surrounded by the shoushan ("longevity hill") motif in the border. This chair cover probably had a contoured companion piece. Wool pile; cotton warp and weft; Senneh knots, 42 per square inch; 3' 5/8" x 3' 1¾" (0.93 m. x 0.96 m.). The Textile Museum, Washington, D.C.

Plate 67
Carpet woven in the nineteenth century displaying the archaic dragon six times: twice in the central roundel and once in each corner. Wool pile; cotton warp and weft; 2' 7½" x 2' 8¼" (0.80 m. x 0.82 m.). Royal Ontario Museum, Toronto, Canada.

Plate 68

■ *Carpet woven between 1736 and 1796 for the emperor Qianlong (an inscription reads* ■
"Qianlong palace fabric"). The theme of the central field is "nine dragons playing in the
sea." In the border are mountain and sea motifs. Wool pile; cotton warp and weft; 9' 4" x
12' 10" (2.87 m. x 3.95 m.). Royal Ontario Museum, Toronto, Canada.
Bequest of Mrs. Frederick W. Cowan.

first and second rank; princes of the third and fourth rank used the four-clawed dragon, princes of the fifth rank, along with certain other high officials, were permitted an emblem of a scaleless serpent-like creature. The power of the dragon had become symbolic of the emperor himself, as an omnipotent being.

As time went on, the dragon continued to receive embellishment until it arrived at more or less its present form. A coded formula developed for representing this fabulous monster that was handed down from masters to apprentices in drawing and painting. The formula for creating the dragon is called "three segments and nine resemblances," the latter referring to the nine specific characteristics that make up the dragon:

1. the head of an ox
2. the horns of a deer
3. eyes like a prawn
4. the snout of a donkey
5. whiskers like a man
6. the ears of a fox
7. the belly of a snake
8. the claws of a phoenix
9. scales like a fish

Carpets usually show the archaic dragon, *kuilong* (Plate 67), sometimes

Evolution of the dragon in Chinese artifacts

Archaic dragon of the Zhou Dynasty

Archaic dragon of the Qin Dynasty

Dragon of the Han Dynasty

Dragon of the Six Dynasties Period

Dragon of the Sui Dynasty

Dragon of the Tang Dynasty

Dragon of the Song Dynasty

Dragon of the Ming Dynasty

Plate 69

■ Pillars in Buddhist prayer halls are often covered with carpets like this one, woven in the
late nineteenth century. Although the dragon appears cut in half in the picture, the body is joined
when it is wrapped around a pillar and looks as
if it were coiling upward. At the bottom is the
shoushan fuhai ("longevity hill-happiness sea")
symbol. At the top are three images of Jiao Tu,
one of the nine sons of the dragon. Wool pile;
cotton warp and weft; Senneh knots, 49 per
square inch, with Ghiordes knots along left edge;
4' ³⁄₈" x 7' 10⅞" (1.23 m. x 2.41 m.). The Textile
Museum, Washington, D.C.

Plate 70

■ Nine Dragon Screen, Forbidden City, Beijing,
near the gate called Jingyunmen. Made of glazed
tiles, these coiling and writhing dragons seem
wonderfully alive, ready to protect the emperor
against all evil spirits.

with a simplified structure. Because the *kuilong* appears frequently as the center disk of a carpet, any center medallion is called *kuilong*, whether it consists of a dragon or a flower. Sometimes the *kuilong* appears in the four corners of a carpet; occasionally it is used in a continuous pattern in the borders. In Plate 58, the archaic dragon alternates with the lotus and *shou* ("longevity") symbols in the border. Besides its use in traditional carpet design, the *kuilong* may figure on temple door curtains, seat and back cushions (Plate 66), and pillar carpets, where the dragon appears to encircle the column (Plate 69).

Traditionally the dragon never wholly reveals himself; just when he seems to come within our grasp he soars into the clouds or dives deep into the sea.[8]

The dragon's reputation for changing shape, size, and color, or making itself visible or invisible, is an ancient belief, and this wonderful creature takes on many forms in Chinese art. This is as it should be, for the dragon is an ever-changing spirit, like the clouds that are its home. In time the supernatural concepts of the fabulous dragon were discarded; by 1911, after the revolution and the overthrow of the Qing Dynasty, even the five-clawed dragon became a common symbol in all Chinese crafts, including carpets. For the people of China, the dragon in its many forms and colors continues to be an important decorative feature as well as a national symbol representing the spirits of change, strength, and perseverance (Plate 70).

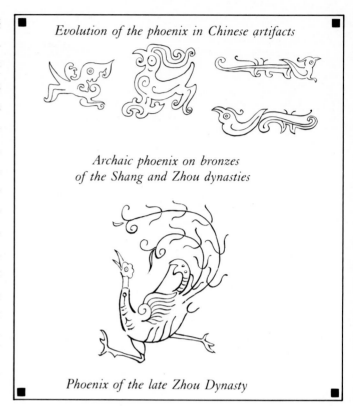

Evolution of the phoenix in Chinese artifacts

Archaic phoenix on bronzes of the Shang and Zhou dynasties

Phoenix of the late Zhou Dynasty

PHOENIX. The phoenix is a familiar creature in many cultures, including the mythologies of ancient Egypt and Greece. In Chinese fairytales and art the phoenix is almost as prominent a motif as the dragon. There is some controversy regarding its sex: the Chinese name for the phoenix is *feng* (凤), and when used in conjunction with the dragon, the *feng* represents the female principle in complement to the maleness of the dragon. *Feng*, however, is correctly applied to the male phoenix and *huang* (凰) to the female. The term *fenghuang* encompasses both sexes.

Like the dragon, the phoenix began as the totem for an early Chinese clan. The name associated with the phoenix clan was Yin, and many phoenix images occur on bronze vessels supposedly cast by the Yin people. There

Phoenix of the Qin and Han dynasties

Phoenix on a bronze mirror of the Qin Dynasty

Phoenix on a bronze mirror of the Han Dynasty

*Phoenix on a tombstone
of the Six Dynasties Period*

Phoenix on a tombstone of the Sui Dynasty

*Phoenix on a tombstone
of the Tang Dynasty*

Phoenix on a stone carving of the Yuan Dynasty

Phoenix on á tomb carving of the Ming Dynasty

Phoenix in embroideries of the Qing Dynasty

is doubt as to which tribal group, the Xia (dragon) or the Yin (phoenix), evolved into the Shang Dynasty, but by that time both beasts were part of the mythological and cultural heritage of the early Chinese.

This mythological creature had a legendary family, five sisters, each of a different color: red, violet, blue, yellow, and black. The phoenix eventually became a symbol of elegance, nobility, peace, and good luck. An old Chinese Classic, *Shanhaijing (Classic of Mountains and Seas)*, describes the phoenix thus: "On Mount Niuchong there was a bird with a plump shape and colored plumes named Luan. She would appear only when the country was at peace." People in general believed that this mythical creature, as a bird of good omen, would only appear when the people lived under a good government. As a sign of good luck, the phoenix decorated many household furnishings, including embroideries, paper-cuts, batiks, and carpets and rugs (Plate 71). On Baotou carpets there were several common patterns, such as *Danfeng Chaoyang* ("a vermillion phoenix faces a sun"), and *Bai Niao Chao Feng* ("a phoenix holds an audience for one hundred birds").

The phoenix also had associations with the ruling class. It became a standard emblem for the empress, whose palaces, vehicles, costumes, headgear, and daily utensils were all decorated with phoenix patterns.

The traditional pattern of the phoenix is graceful, exquisite, and refined. It first appeared on Shang bronze vessels and later adorned silk paintings of the Warring States Period. At that time the archaic phoenix in ceramics and stone carvings was simple in shape, but through the ages the composition became more complicated. Like the dragon, the phoenix design developed into a formula for artists to follow:

1. the throat of a swallow
2. the bill of a fowl
3. the neck of a snake
4. the tail of a fish
5. the forehead of a crane
6. the crown of a mandarin drake
7. the scales of a dragon
8. the vaulted back of a tortoise

The phoenix is said to "resemble a wild swan before, and a unicorn behind." The feathers were in five colors, named after the cardinal virtues of Confucian philosophy: human-heartedness, righteousness, altruism, integrity, and good faith.

Plate 71 (opposite above)
■ *A phoenix with wings displayed as a circle forms the central medallion of this fine early nineteenth-century carpet. Peonies are dotted on the field and four more phoenixes fill the corners. Wool pile; cotton warp and weft; Senneh knots, 33 per square inch; 5' 4 ⅝" x 8' 2⅜" (1.64 m. x 2.50 m.). The Textile Museum, Washington, D.C.* ■

Plate 72 (opposite below)
■ *Carpet woven in the eighteenth century. The field of this rug represents the sky full of cranes and bats in flight. Wool pile; cotton warp and weft; Senneh knots, 33 per square inch; 5' 4¼" x 8' 9½" (1.63 m. x 2.68 m.). The Textile Museum, Washington, D.C. Gift of George Hewitt Myers.* ■

Many symbols, especially specific groupings of symbols, come directly from the three major Chinese religion-philosophies, Taoism, Confucianism, and Chinese Buddhism.

could exert any influence on it. It r volved continuously. It could be rec oned as the foundation from whi all worldly things were created. I not know its name, just call it *dao*.

The Eight Immortals of Taoism

TAOISM. Taoism takes its name from the extremely important idea or concept *dao* (道), which is usually translated as "the way," that refers to the means by which one finds peace, achieves harmony with the universe, finds longevity, or even discovers the secret to immortality.

According to the original author of *Daodejing (Book of the Power of the Way)*, the Taoist bible, "There exists an integral whole prior to the formation of the Heaven and Earth, noiseless and shapeless; no external forces

Taoist mythology centers around t stories of eight immortal beings wh enjoyed unlimited lives of great hap ness in a world beyond human exis ence. Desires that could not be satisfi in a human's life become possible this other world. The legends are elaboration of the meditative princ ples of Laozi,[10] which taught man reach inside himself and find true fu fillment by rising above the concer of secular existence.

The legend of the Eight Immorta has been current for centuries in Ch

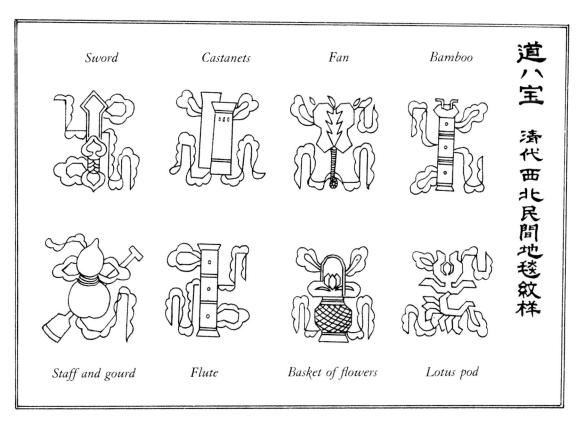

道八宝　清代西北民間地毯紋样

Sword　　Castanets　　Fan　　Bamboo

Staff and gourd　　Flute　　Basket of flowers　　Lotus pod

The Eight Treasures of Taoism in archaic and modern styles

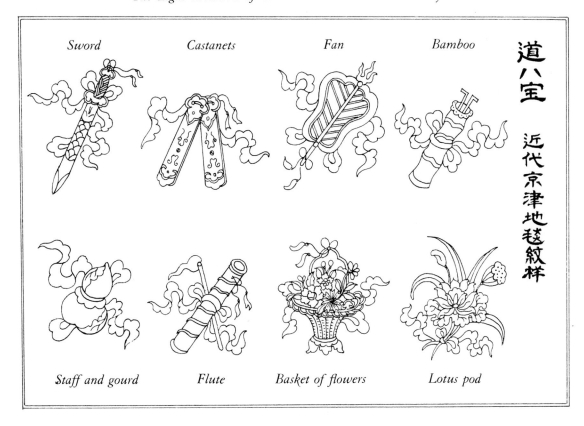

道八宝　近代京津地毯紋样

Sword　　Castanets　　Fan　　Bamboo

Staff and gourd　　Flute　　Basket of flowers　　Lotus pod

Plate 73

■ *Carpet woven in Shanghai in 1981. Around the central medallion are placed the* ■
four symbols of the Confucian gentleman: harp, chessboard, scrolls, and books. The
outer border displays a selection of Buddhist Treasures motifs: wheel, fish, flower,
canopy, umbrella, and conch shell. The pattern is often called Meeting of Philoso-
phy and Religion. Wool pile; cotton warp and weft; Senneh knots; 6' x 9'
(1.83 m. x 2.74 m.).

Plate 74
■ *Carpet woven in Shanghai in 1982. The symbols include bamboo, whose message is* ■
"good luck," and peonies, emblematic of riches and honor. Wool pile; cotton warp and
weft; Senneh knots, 90-line quality; 6' x 9' (1.83 m. x 2.74 m.).

nese folklore and plays. It is difficult to trace its exact history because, as in most legends, names and details changed frequently as they passed through the generations. The Immortals were mentioned briefly in books of the Song, Yuan, and Ming dynasties.

An author of the Ming period named Wu Yuantai described eight specific personages who have come to be known as the Eight Immortals of Taoism. Later, plays and stories such as "Eight Immortals Celebrate a Birthday," "Eight Immortals Cross the Sea," and "Eight Drunken Immortals" became popular.

The Eight Immortals rarely appear in carpet patterns, for the weaving of human forms into a pile carpet is a difficult process with danger of distortion. However, each of the Immortals is known to carry a specific article, and these often appear in carpet patterns. They are usually called the Eight Treasures of Taoism: sword, castanets, fan, bamboo, staff and gourd, flute, basket of flowers, and lotus pod.

CONFUCIANISM. Concurrently with the idealistic philosophy of Laozi was established another major philosophy in China, one which most Westerners know at least by name, Confucianism. The first preacher of this philosophy was Kong Qiu, a great thinker and teacher who became revered as his philosophy was glorified by successive generations of followers, and he was addressed out of respect as Kong Fuzi (孔夫子). In medieval times this name was Latinized into Confucius when his name and teach-

ings were introduced to the West by travelers, priests, and merchants.

Confucianism considered human-heartedness, or *ren* (仁), to be the most effective power toward achieving harmony on earth, and teaching and scholarship to be the means toward attaining an ideal society, based on social organization and responsibility.

Harp   *Chessboard*

Books   *Scrolls*

Confucian symbols representing refinement, elegance, and great learning

The four main symbols of Confucianism are harp, chessboard, books, and scrolls. These objects are connected with Confucian teaching because they are emblematic of the scholar's life. The four symbols often appear together on Chinese carpets and represent qualities important to the Confucian gentleman (Plate 73).

The Chinese harp is usually pictured in carpet design as half enclosed in a bag; the chessboard is simplified for the weaver into a board with only a few squares, sometimes accompanied by two containers for chessmen. The four objects are often tied with ornamental ribbons that seem to flutter in the breeze.

BUDDHISM. The introduction of Buddhism from India to China occurred in the middle of the first century A.D., for the first note about it is found in Chinese historical records in 67 A.D., during the reign of Mingdi of the Eastern Han Dynasty. Early in the fifth century, Buddhist leaders were wise enough to link their religion with Confucian ritualism, which eased its development into a major element in Chinese civilization. Buddhism takes many forms, and the Chinese were quick to incorporate Buddhism into a system of belief more Chinese than Indian.

upon a stone with his face to the south. His footprints were left there for posterity and on these imprints appear eight lucky emblems of Buddhism, symbols of all that is happy and good. Two of these, the lotus and the fish, have already been discussed.

1. *Wheel*: This most important Buddhist symbol represents to perfection the cyclical view of life that is at the heart of Buddhist teachings. The Wheel of the Law refers to the concept of karma; it is said that the Buddha sat under a linden tree with a wheel model in his hand as

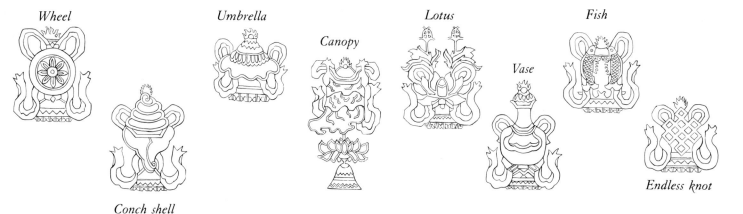

Wheel

Umbrella

Canopy

Lotus

Vase

Fish

Conch shell

Endless knot

The Eight Treasures of Buddhism

Buddhism, like Taoism, was stronger in certain periods of Chinese history and less favored in others. It has had a continuing influence on Chinese art, and many of the symbols already discussed derived some of their meaning from Chinese Buddhism. Several objects closely associated with Buddhism are sometimes seen in pattern groupings in Chinese carpet designs, such as the Eight Treasures of Buddhism (Plates 39, 40).

According to legend, the Buddha went to Kusinara in 487 B.C. and stood

he taught his pupils about the principle of cause and effect in life. The turning wheel, which never ceases, is referred to as the Wheel of Birth and Death. The goal of the Buddhist is to emancipate himself from the cycle by rising above and beyond it, to achieve the state called Nirvana.

2. *Conch shell*: The whorls of the shell symbolize a prosperous journey. Like all the Buddhist Treasures, the shell is a symbol of good luck, but it can also represent royalty.

3. *Umbrella:* Also called the state umbrella, it is an emblem of authority. The symbolic analogy is to the protection of the state, which shelters the masses.

4. *Canopy:* An elaborate form of the umbrella, the canopy is a symbol of official rank.

5. *Lotus:* Probably the most common Buddhist symbol, the lotus is regarded as a sacred flower, the emblem of purity. Painted and sculptured figures of Buddha are often seated on the petals of a lotus, the so-called Sumeru Seat.

6. *Vase:* The vase, also known as the precious vase, is a receptacle for achievements and virtue.

7. *Fish:* In pairs, fish are considered an emblem of wealth, abundance, faithfulness, and marital happiness. The carp also represents the qualities of strength, speed, and the ability to escape unscathed from a calamity.

8. *Knot:* The knot is a coil of endless knots that symbolizes longevity and eternity. The endlessly twisting coil, with no beginning or end, suggests the illumination of the soul by the mysteries of the universe.

It is difficult to describe specifically the three major philosophies of China because they continued to change throughout the country's long history. The major tenets of Buddhism, at first a foreign idea, were almost immediately redefined in Chinese, usually Taoist, terms. Centuries after Confucianism, Taoism, and Buddhism had been established, a philosophy emerged in the Song Dynasty called Neo-Confucianism. A synthesis of much of the Buddhist, Taoist, and Confucian vocabularies, Neo-Confucianism is not simply eclectic, but an attempt to unify the principles of these great philosophies into a consistent whole.[11]

Plate 75
■ *This carpet, called a Friendship Rug, was woven in Shanghai in 1977. The central medallion shows two versions of the* shou *emblem, and the border displays two more. The restrained use of these symbols creates an elegant carpet design. Wool pile; cotton warp and weft; Senneh knots, 90-line quality; 6' x 9' (1.83 m. x 2.74 m.).* ■

Plate 76

■ *The seat mat and seat back shown above were woven in Baotou, Inner Mongolia, in the late nineteenth century. The* wan *symbol in the center of the seat mat (below) wishes the lama who used it "ten thousand years." The wish is repeated in the second border by the endless-knot motif. Here the* wans *turn their crampons in both directions. The outer border has archaic dragons, and dragons in their ancient geometric form fill the corners of the central field. The seat back has the same border of archaic dragons and includes motifs selected from the Buddhist Treasures and Taoist Treasures. Wool pile; cotton warp and weft; 2' 3⅞" x 2' 3⅞" (0.716 m. x 0.716 m.). Whereabouts unknown.* ■

WAN. In China this geometrical design means "ten thousand" (Plate 76). Although some later associations connected with Taoism claimed this diagram as their emblem, it is not really Taoist. It is believed that the symbol was first borrowed from India, where it is regarded as the "seal of Buddha's heart"; it is often placed on the heart of Sakyamuni (historic) Buddha images.

This symbol is frequent in ancient cultures, and many archaeologists believe it originated as a representation of the sun's course in the heavens. The English name for the symbol, swastika, is taken from the ancient Sanskrit meaning "well-being." Although it is customarily held that the Chinese *wan* symbol is a mirror image of the Nazi swastika, in fact the symbol in Chinese carpets turns its crampons in both clockwise and counterclockwise directions.

The Chinese name for the symbol was coined in 693 by edict of Wu Zetian (624–705), empress of the Tang Dynasty (regent 684–690; empress 690–704). Wu Zetian reportedly invented eighteen other words during her reign. This act was thought exceedingly bold, for the privilege of coining words was considered to belong only to sages of the past.

The *wan* symbol usually appears in a connected pattern on the borders of carpets, a border pattern emblematic of endless wealth and a continuous rise through the official ranks of the court.

FRET AND MEANDER. These figures found in border patterns of carpets may take many shapes, usually geometric, including the connecting *wan* symbol. The winding patterns signify long life and unending happiness.

One fret pattern, very ancient, is called *leiwen* (雷纹), or "thunder pattern." The *leiwen* first appeared on prehistoric pottery and later on Shang and Zhou bronzes.

SHOU. The *shou* character symbol, one of the most common on Chinese carpets, represents old age and longevity. These qualities, so admired and revered in Chinese culture, are reflections of the Taoist search for immortality and the Confucian regard for the wisdom of age.

The *shou*, when it appears alone in carpets, is often a round form, sometimes elaborately displayed as a central medallion (Plate 55). An elongated, open form also occurs in carpets, occasionally as a pattern repeated in the border (Plate 75).

Centuries ago Chinese calligraphers wrote one hundred forms of *shou* in a design on one sheet of paper, intended as a gift expressing the wish that the recipient would "live to be a centenarian" (see page 88).

XI. This character symbol (the word *xi* means "happiness") represents a joyful and jubilant spirit, and a pair of these symbols is emblematic of wedded bliss. A carpet with a series of double *xi* patterns would mean "double happiness," a most appropriate gift for a newly married couple.

Fret and meander border designs. Variations of the wan *symbol are interlaced with hook and T motifs.*

Two forms of leiwen.

Six forms of shou: *three round, three elongated*

Two forms of xi

COINS. Money is often represented in Chinese rug designs. The earliest Chinese coins were knife- or trouser-shaped. Disk-shaped coins with a square hole in the center were first made in the Qin Dynasty and continued almost unchanged into the Qing Dynasty. The hole was for stringing to facilitate carrying them, and its square shape embodied the ancient idea of the universe—"a square earth enveloped within a spherical heaven." The most familiar copper coin in Chinese numismatic history is the *wuzhu* (五铢), normally weighing about one third of an ounce, which first appeared during Wudi's reign in the Han Dynasty. The obvious significance of the coin motif is "prosperity," and coins are sometimes worn as jewelry or good-luck charms. In a carpet pattern, coins may appear singly, in connected pairs, or in a continual chain (Plate 65).

JI. The *ji* (戟), or trident, is an ancient iron weapon with a long handle used for pricking and chopping (Plate 60). Its usual symbolism is a homophonic one, the pronunciation of *ji* being similar to the Chinese words for "good omen" (吉) and "grade" (级).

BOGU: *A GRAND COLLECTION OF ANTIQUES.* The Song emperor Zhaoji (ruled 1101–1125) decided that a pictorial catalog should be made of all the precious antique objects stored in the palace treasury. The emperor himself was a noted painter, and he instructed the professional painters of the Imperial Gallery to represent the ancient collection on scrolls. This re-quired thirty scrolls, which are called *Xuanhe Bogu Tu* (宣和博古图), meaning "collection of antiques in the years of Xuanhe," and from that time any painting of ancient art objects was called *Bogu.*

The *bogu* objects in carpet patterns are usually bronze vessels or jade and porcelain articles. The spaces between the antiques are sometimes filled with decorative plants, flowers, fruits, and vegetables.

SCENERY. Landscape motifs are sometimes part of the design patterns of Chinese rugs. One such design is called *Shoushan,* "longevity hill." Mount Shou is a real mountain about 60 *li* (19 miles) north of Fuzhou, capital of Fujian Province. Stones with strange forms and attractive colors are often excavated there, and rocks from Mount Shou naturally carry with them the significance of longevity.

Fuhai is the "happiness sea" design. Since the sea is considered boundless, *fuhai* presents the concept of happiness and wisdom that have no limits. Early carpets (Plate 69) often combined "longevity hill" with "happiness sea": *shoushan fuhai* (寿 山福海).

Mountain and sea symbol (shoushan fuhai)

Plate 77

■ *Carpet woven in Shanghai in 1976. The pictorial style became popular in the 1920s. Typical of such designs are the camel-back bridges and pagodas evocative of the Chinese landscape to Western eyes. The pattern is called West Lake at Hangzhou, Zhejiang. Wool pile; cotton warp and weft; Senneh knots, 90-line quality; 6' x 9' (1.83 m. x 2.74 m.).* ■

A particular rug pattern may include combinations of several complementary motifs, some of them traditional combinations that communicate fairly complex messages. Since the Chinese approach to rug design has usually been message-oriented rather than strictly aesthetic, the possibilities of meaning in a design are limited only by the designer's capacity for putting new motifs together to form new ideas. (By no means are all the designs that are now or have ever been used in Chinese rugs included here.) Certain patterns are traditional favorites, however, and in the following section some of these patterns are described. Many consist of motifs that have already been discussed, others include new motifs. The complexity of these designs begins to show just how much of an adventure a Chinese rug can be!

BATS AND COINS. A design consisting of these two symbols means "happiness is right before your eyes" (福在眼前).

bat	*(fu)*	happiness
coin	*(qian)*	before
hole	*(yan)*	eye (hole of coin)

FIVE BATS ENCIRCLING A ROUNDED SHOU *EMBLEM.* This configuration means *wufu pengshou* (五福捧寿), which can be translated as "five bats lift up longevity." The number of bats is significant because they represent the Five Blessings: long life, wealth, health and peace, love of virtue, and a natural death. (*Peng* means to lift something up with both hands; *shou*, of course, signifies "long life.")

BAT WITH THREE PEACHES. Like the *shou* symbol, the peach is an emblem of longevity. A motif combining a bat and peaches conveys the message of enjoying both happiness and long life (see page 193).

PEACH, BUDDHA'S HAND, AND A POMEGRANATE. These three figures signify abundant happiness (as from a prosperous family), official honor, and long life (see page 193).

PINE, BAMBOO, AND PLUM.
When in one composite pattern, these three symbols represent bosom friends who can stand the test of time. This meaning comes from an old Chinese phrase, "three friends in chilly weather," or *suihan sanyou* (岁寒三友). The pine and bamboo are evergreens and withstand winter; plum trees bloom when the weather is still cold.

PLUM, BAMBOO, CHRYSAN-THEMUM, AND ORCHID. This quartet is called *si junzi* (四君子), or "four men of noble character."

CRANE, STAG, AND TOON TREE.
This combination means *helu tongchun* (鹤鹿同春), "a wish for an official promotion in springtime."

he	crane, first-degree official
lu	white-spotted deer, official wages
tong	toon tree, "together"
chun	germination, budding in spring

In a carpet, the pattern usually depicts a crane with a stag in the foreground and a toon tree (*cedrela toona*) beside the stag. Many old Baotou rugs include this grouping (Plate 78).

CRANE STANDING IN A RISING TIDE. This combination signifies the wish to become an official of the first degree in the royal court: *yipin dangchao* (一品当朝).

yipin	first-degree official (symbolized by a crane)
dang	facing
chao	tide, the royal court

FUNGUS IN A VASE ON A TABLE.
These symbols can be read as *ping'an ruyi* (平安如意), signifying "safe and secure as you wish it."

vase (*ping*)	safe and secure
table (*an*)	safety
fungus (*ruyi*)	"as you wish it"

THREE JI IN A VASE. This grouping signifies a promotion of three official degrees, *ping sheng sanji* (平升三级).

ping	vase, straight up
sheng	raise
san	three
ji	degree

EGRET, LOTUS, AND WITH-ERED LOTUS LEAF. Here the implied wish is *yilu lian ke*, "a series of successful examinations for the official post" (Plate 79).

yilu lian	a series of
lu	egret
lian	lotus growing from its root
ke	official post (symbolized by the withered lotus leaf)

Plate 78

*Carpet woven in Baotou, Inner Mongolia, probably early in the twenti-
eth century. In this rendition of the crane, stag, and toon-tree pattern,
the tree is very stylized. Wool pile; cotton warp and weft; Senneh knots,
36 per square inch; 2' x 3' 4⅛" (0.61 m. x 1.02 m.). The Textile
Museum, Washington, D.C. Gift of Dr. William H. S. Stevens.*

Plate 79

Carpet woven in the eighteenth century to serve as a chair mat or throne cover. Within a tan border with blue corner scrolls, a white egret stands in a lotus pool, symbolizing the wish of poor parents to have their son rise up through the ranks of officialdom to a high post. Wool pile; cotton warp and weft; Senneh knots, 56 per square inch; 3' 3¾" x 3'6⅛" (1.01 m. x 1.07 m.). The Textile Museum, Washington, D.C.

Color Symbolism

Color contributes its appropriate meanings and purposes to Chinese symbolism and may signify rank, authority, virtues and vices, or joys and sorrows. According to the ancient Chinese system, the five primary colors are red, yellow, blue (which includes green), white, and black.

Red is the emblem of joy, and is employed for all festive occasions, especially marriage.

Yellow was made the national color in the Qing Dynasty, and was sacred to the emperor and assumed only by himself and his sons, or by lineal descendants of his family.

Purple, or violet, is the color of majesty and dignity.

White is the color of mourning.

Blue is the color of serenity and purity.

Black is the sign of evil.

Color symbolism also indicates the points of the compass: east, according to the Classics, must be blue; west is white; north is black; and south is red.

In the Chinese theater, a red face usually denotes a sacred person; a black face, a rough but honest man; a white face indicates a treacherous, cunning, but dignified person; a mean fellow or low comedian is given a white nose.

---

[1] Yu-lan Fung, *A Short History of Chinese Philosophy*, ed. Derk Bodde, New York, 1948, p. 253.

[2] In Tibet, most of the lamas were illiterate, and instead of chanting the sutra during Lamaist services the lamas turned a bronze cylinder, the surface of which bore engraved sutra chapters and the six-word code *on ma ni bai mei hong* (meaning "the precious seat is in a lotus"). This code stood for the sutra texts, and its continued repetition was regarded as efficacious against all pernicious influences.

[3] Soame Jenyns, *A Background to Chinese Painting*, New York, 1966, p. 196.

[4] *Ibid.*, p. 197.

[5] Michael Sullivan, *Chinese and Japanese Art*, London, 1965, p. 48.

[6] Four are in the Xi'an Museum, Shaanxi, two are in the University Museum in Philadelphia. They are believed to have been sculptured in 636 A.D.

[7] Kakuzo Okakura, *The Awakening of Japan*, New York, 1905, pp. 77–78.

[8] Sullivan, *Chinese and Japanese Art*, p. 65.

[9] Chapter 34.

[10] Traditionally, a scholar and sage at the Zhou court, born at the end of the seventh century B.C.

[11] Fung, *A Short History of Chinese Philosophy*, p. 269.

3. WEAVING METHODS AND TECHNIQUES

Plate 80

Antique Finish carpet made in Inner Mongolia in 1979. A traditional embroidery-like design was selected for this modern carpet. Four borders surround the central field. The first displays a row of pearls, the second a meander pattern, and the third endless knots. The fourth is a solid blue band. Wool pile; cotton warp and weft; Senneh knots, 90-line quality; 4' x 6' (1.22 m. x 1.83 m.).

Plate 81

Detail of a carpet woven in the early nineteenth century. This all-over floral design is related to textile patterns. The vegetable dyes have faded, except for the indigo blue. Wool pile; cotton warp and weft; Senneh knots, 33 per square inch; 6' x 15' 2¾" (1.83 m. x 4.65 m.). The Textile Museum, Washington, D.C.

Plate 82
■ *Weaver at a loom in an eastern factory.* ■

Chinese hand-knotted pile carpets and rugs belong to a traditional art form that developed over many centuries in several different regions of China. Each rug demands time, care, and craftsmanship, and carpet experts throughout the world rate Chinese carpets above others for their quality and aesthetic standards.

Many types and varieties of hand-knotted carpets are made in China. Today the largest production centers are in the eastern part of the country, in Tianjin, Beijing, Shanghai, and other municipalities and provinces. Elsewhere in China, especially in the western regions, different types of handmade and hand-knotted carpets are produced. In the autonomous regions, where carpets have been woven for thousands of years, the weavers continue to use many of the same motifs and styles that appear in ancient rugs.

Except in the western autonomous regions, where the terminology is somewhat different, most of the carpet production in China is described by the number of "lines" per foot of width. These lines are actually the method of counting the vertical "warps," the cotton threads stretched in pairs from the top beam of the loom to the bottom beam. For example, when a 90-line carpet is to be woven 6 feet wide, 1,080 warps will be stretched from the top to the bottom of the loom, representing 6 times 180 threads, or 90 pairs of warps for each foot of car-

pet width. The carpet so woven is described as being of 90-line quality.

The majority of carpets woven in China are of 90-line quality, and the 90-line is the standard by which most Chinese carpets are judged. Other qualities of carpets—70-line, 80-line, 120-line—are not uncommon, and carpets with even higher knottage counts are woven. Among the finest carpets in the world are intricately knotted Chinese carpets of 150-line, 200-line, and even 300-line quality.

Many steps go into the process of manufacturing Chinese hand-knotted pile carpets. The chart below illustrates the processes, and how they are related to one another.

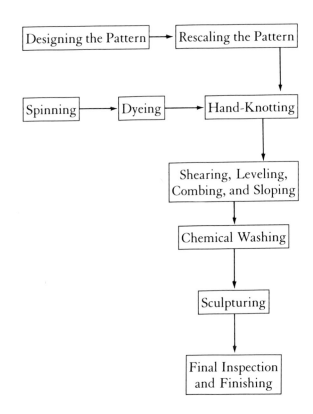

Plate 83
An artist in a modern factory in Tianjin is designing a carpet pattern.

DESIGNING THE PATTERN. The art of carpet weaving has been passed down from generation to generation for centuries, and until the beginning of the twentieth century, Chinese artisans wove their carpets without using preliminary sketches. A master weaver knew how and when to make the knots that would bring into being the perfect flower, bird, or other motif. Only when carpet production was expanded for commerce and export did weavers start to use designs from paper patterns. Patterns are now designed by special artists who are trained for this specific job at de-sign institutes. The weavers, working in large factories, use the intricate hand-knotting techniques to execute the artists' patterns.

A large number of designs have been committed to paper in the past thirty years, and now over 3,000 designs are available in China.

An artist first accumulates source materials and thinks out the design in preliminary drawings. His final sketch is made on a sheet of paper measuring 10½ by 14 inches, approximately one tenth the size of a 9- by 12-foot rug. The design is painted in gouache colors.

Plate 84

■ *Carpet woven in Shanghai in 1979. The motifs include peonies, symbolizing spring,* ■
riches, and honor, and plum blossoms, symbolizing winter and fortitude. Baskets of flowers
in the border are interesting and unusual elements in this type of design. Wool pile; cotton
warp and weft; Senneh knots, 90-line quality; 6' x 9' (1.83 m. x 2.74 m.).

RESCALING THE PATTERN. When the gouache drawing has been approved, then a sketch or cartoon to the actual size of the carpet is drawn —not in color, but in outline. This cartoon is fixed behind the warp screen, close enough to be seen through the threads (Plate 85). As the weaver begins to tie knots and thus begin the weaving process, he or she carefully traces with red ink the outline of the design onto the warp threads.

The rescaling process is not a simple reproduction in the manner of a photographic enlargement or reduction. The form and style of the original design must be maintained and the aesthetic arrangement of the composition must not deviate too much from it. Carpets of different sizes and shapes need to be made as an enlargement or reduction of the design, and care is needed to adapt the composition in each case.

In creating a design for each size of carpet, the artist must also prejudge the shrinkage of the cotton threads that will occur when the carpet is chemically washed. Both the warp and the weft are of cotton, and they may shrink at different rates; the artist designs the cartoons in such a way that no irregularity in the appearance of the pattern will result from the washing.

Chinese designers of carpets, who enlarge, reduce, or modify their designs for various sizes and shapes of carpet, must be true artists in their sense of proportion, well versed in Chinese folklore, and fully trained in the Chinese classical traditions of the fine arts. They have also studied and understood all of the weaving techniques and methods used in the production of carpets, including the hand-knotting process, dyeing, the use of color, and the processes of chemical washing, as well as the total effect that a carpet will present after completion—this must all be familiar to them before they can create the designs and arrange the colors.

SPINNING THE YARN. Machine-spun woolen yarns are used for the pile of virtually all hand-knotted rugs made in China today. Until the end of the nineteenth century, Chinese carpets were made of hand-spun yarn. When spinning machines began to arrive in China early in the twentieth century, the changeover to the superior machine-spun yarns was slow and gradual. Today, hand-spun yarns are only used for carpets made in the autonomous regions, where the traditional ethnic style still requires them.

Machine-spun yarns, in addition to uniformity, have greater tensile strength. Several types of Chinese wool are first blended together to make carpet wool. The wool is then washed by a careful process to remove natural fats, grease, and foreign matter. After the washing the fibers are carded and then spun through a series of spinning processes to produce the proper "yarn count" (see below) for each type of carpet.

Out of these woolen yarns is made the pile of the carpet. "Pile" is the word for the "nap" or surface above the backing; in a pile carpet, this is a vertical stand of woolen yarns packed close together like blades of grass in a lawn.

A word about yarn counts will clarify this method of describing woolen yarns. The strand of yarn in one kilogram of a 3.5-count yarn, such as that used in a 90-line carpet, is 3,500 meters long. This is a finer yarn than that used in a 70-line carpet, which requires 2.5-count yarn, 2,500 meters in length of strand, and weighing one kilogram. Other examples of the finer yarns are the 120-line carpet using 6-count, the 150-line using 7.5-count, and the 200-line and up using 8-count yarns. In all cases the warps and wefts are cotton, usually of 10-count cotton thread.

The word "ply" describes the number of single strands of yarn that are twisted together to make a "plied" yarn. Such composite strands of yarn, of course, have more tensile strength and are more durable than single-strand yarns.

DYEING THE YARN. The unique coloration that captures everyone's eye when viewing a Chinese rug is achieved with the use of dyes. The designs in Chinese woolen carpets often include interpretations of natural objects, and a living plant, for example, requires an astounding number of colors to show its various parts, such as flowers and buds, leaves and new shoots, branches, and stamen and pistils. In addition to the variety of colors, a good number of shades of each color are needed. To attain these effects, the Chinese woolen carpet industry has established more than 600 different colors and shades, all maintained in the yarn inventories of the major factories in China. (For the making of tapestries, more than 1,200 colors have been defined.) All of these colors are numbered and are used throughout China except in certain autonomous regions, where ethnic minorities retain their own preferences for color.

Before the use of aniline dyes became known in China, there were vegetable dyes. Vegetable dyeing is a laborious process and, with some exceptions, there is no sure way of insuring uniformity of color, complete stability, or fastness of color. The merits of vegetable dyes, however, appeal to collectors and admirers of antique carpets, for vegetable dyes give a serene, soft appearance to carpet yarns. Certain vegetable dyes, such as indigo, have a satisfactory fastness of color, and, today, a type of fine carpet called Antique Finish is made in China with vegetable dyes (Plate 80). Chrome (chemical) dyes are now used throughout the world, and the Chinese carpet industry is the only one we know that intentionally continues the use of vegetable dyes for one or two specific types of carpet. No other dyes provide this "look." The vegetable dyeing of woolen hand-knotted carpets can be traced back many thousands of years. The colored carpet fragments discovered at the Normhong River site and among the Niya relics provide clear evidence of the early use of vegetable dyes in China.

An ancient book called *Grand Encyclopedia of Yongle (Yongle Dadian,* 永乐大典),[1] published between 1403 and 1408 A.D., describes actual carpet

Plate 85

■ *An enlarged design (full size) is mounted behind the warps of a carpet in production.* ■

Plate 86

■ *Spinning cotton into threads for warps and wefts is done today by machine.*
When a spindle is completely wound with yarn it is removed and another is put
in its place. If the thread breaks, it is tied together by the machine operator. ■

Plate 87
In this view of a factory in Shanghai, dyed yarn is being carried to the drying room by the man in the background.

Plate 88
The modern carpet weaver has almost limitless shades of colored yarn at his disposal.

Plate 89

■ *Some sources of vegetable dyes are (from left to right) madder roots, acorn cups, and seed* ■
husks of sophora japonica.

production. It states that between 1279 and 1290 A.D., in making a certain lot of five pieces of carpet with a total surface area of 992.83 square *chi* (about 1,185 square feet), the consumption of vegetable dyes amounted to over 1,300 *jin* (more than 1,433 pounds). These figures indicate the grand scale of production in those days.

Vegetable and mineral dyes may have more than a hundred sources in plants, bark, nutshells, berries, and insects. Since the fifteenth century, carpet makers in the household workshops in northwestern China prepared the most common basic colors, blue, yellow, red, tan, and black and from these colors made mixtures and gradations through combination:

1. Blue, from the indigo plant *(polygonum tinctorum)*. This plant produces four shades of blue: dark, medium, cerulean, and pale.

2. Yellow, obtained from weld or the buds of *sophora japonica* and the seed husks of *gardenia jasminoides*. Three gradations of yellow are produced.
3. Purplish red, from sumac.
4. Terra-cotta red, from madder roots *(rubia tinctorum)*.
5. Light brown or tan, from acorn cups.
6. Black, from pomegranate peels, or from flour broth, with the addition of iron rust.
7. Yellowish green or bluish green, obtained by adding indigo blue to *sophora* yellow.
8. Apricot, made by mixing madder-root red with *sophora* yellow. By adjusting the proportions of these, rusty red can also be obtained.
9. Deep violet, obtained by mixing acorn-cup tan with some pomegranate black.

Indigo blue is a direct color: yarn dipped in a solution containing indigo

146

Plate 90
■ *Weavers at a modern metal loom.* ■

is dyed blue after a given amount of time, and no further treatment is needed to fix the color permanently. Other vegetable dyes require a mordant chemical to stabilize the colors. Alum, blue vitriol, potassium bichromate, and tannin (obtained from walnuts) are used to stabilize such vegetable dyes as red and orange; aluminum salt is used for yellow.

Many very old Chinese carpets appear to be woven of tan and blue yarn because indigo dye is almost completely colorfast while other dyes fade, and wool dyed yellow often softens into tan (Plate 81). Because it is a direct color, indigo blue eventually becomes blue-black as it oxidizes from exposure to air. Woolen yarns dyed with indigo blue also become tougher and stronger, and stand up better to abrasion than do yarns dyed with other colors. Pile dyed with other colors may show excessive wear, apparently a result of the tendency of some dyes to attack the woolen yarn, causing it to lose its natural qualities and become brittle; the fiber then breaks and disappears, thus "wearing out" more quickly. Vitriol, too, can weaken fibers. In old carpets certain yarns appear to be worn down to the fabric back while others, such as those dyed with indigo, appear fresh, flexible, and lustrous.

147

Plate 91 (opposite)
■ *Weavers at an old-fashioned loom in Urumqi,* ■
Xinjiang.

Plate 92
■ *In this sample of wool pile-knotting, the* ■
bird's eye is tied with a Ghiordes, or horse-
shoe, knot.

Plate 93
■ *Weavers at a modern metal loom.* ■

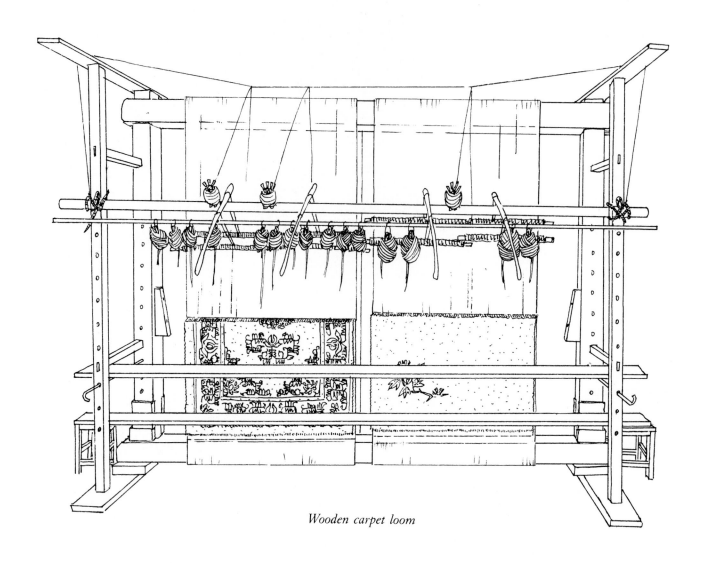

Wooden carpet loom

The Chinese industry today uses chemical dyes to guarantee the quality of the dyed wool and to fulfill the prime requirements in dyeing: that colors will be both uniform and fast, except sometimes in the most direct, bright sunlight. The chemical dyes used today are applied in a time-honored, proven process that allows the carpet to stand up later under the rough treatment of chemical washing. Chemical washing and scrubbing give a high luster to the wool pile, and no other dyes are known to be capable of sustaining the washing treatment without losing color. This fastness of color in the washing process and in subsequent use comes from precipitation on the woolen fibers of basic salt in the dye that is not soluble in water or in the chemicals used in the washing process.

HAND-KNOTTING OR WEAVING THE CARPET. Hand-knotting is the most important phase of carpet making, for it demands all the artistry that the weaver can supply and it gives Chinese carpets their distinctive character. The Chinese weaver's skill is paramount in producing a carpet; great dexterity, speed, precision, patience, and sensitivity are the traits of master Chinese weavers.

The warp yarns of cotton are stretched tightly from the top beam of the loom to the bottom beam. These warps are the foundation on which the pile yarn is knotted. To start the weaving process and create a base for knotting the first line of pile yarn, several "shots" of weft thread are passed through the warps and are pounded down tightly until a strong base, or selvage, has been formed. (The movement of a weft thread in one direction over and under each alternate warp thread is called a shot.) Upon this base, the first row of pile yarn is knotted, followed by two new weft threads, inserted and pounded down separately with an iron comb made specially for this purpose. Row by row this process continues, until the carpet is completed.

The pile yarns in the main body of the carpet are looped around two warps to make a knot resembling a figure 8. This knot is commonly known as the Persian, or Senneh, knot. Another type of knot used is known as the Turkish, or Ghiordes, knot, though in China it is referred to as the horseshoe knot. Sometimes it is used for making small elements in the design, such as birds' eyes, in order to achieve a naturally round effect (Plate 92).

It is interesting to note that the pile does not stand straight up, but instead leans in one direction, which makes the color of the carpet look lighter when viewed from one side and darker from the other. The fibers' reflection and absorption of light cause this phenomenon. Light is reflected from the surface of the yarn when the viewer stands at the "light" side of the carpet because the pile is leaning away from him and reflecting light; when the viewer stands at the "dark" side, he is looking into the ends of the pile yarn, which lean toward him and absorb the light.

Plate 94
Chemical washing in an eastern factory.

Plate 95
Some tools used by weavers are (from right to left) scissors, weft dabber, and cutting knife.

Plate 96
■ *One of the steps in chemical washing is* ■
scrubbing the pile.

Plate 97
■ *Sculpturing the carpet in an eastern factory.* ■

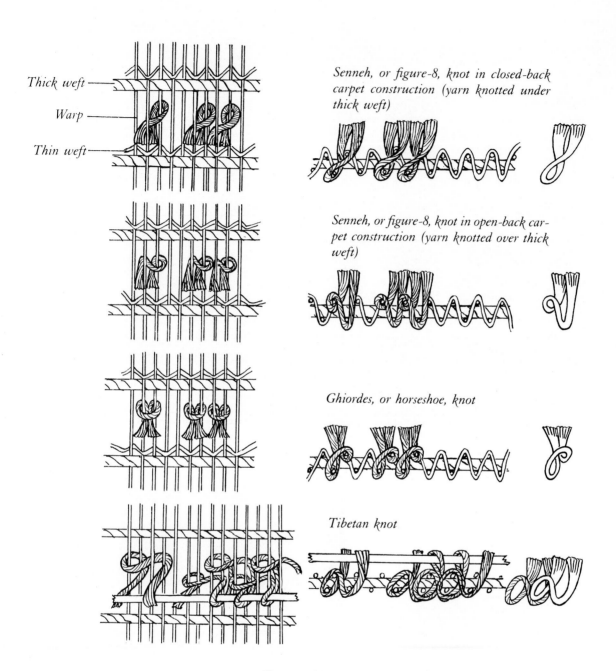

Thick weft

Warp

Thin weft

Senneh, or figure-8, knot in closed-back carpet construction (yarn knotted under thick weft)

Senneh, or figure-8, knot in open-back carpet construction (yarn knotted over thick weft)

Ghiordes, or horseshoe, knot

Tibetan knot

Knots used in weaving Chinese pile carpets

When one looks horizontally along the weft or vertically along the warp, the knots are always in a straight line, but in following a curve in the pattern the knots must form a zigzag design along the horizontal and vertical wefts and warps, like steps on a staircase. If one realizes that each knot occupies one fiftieth of a square inch (1.1 square millimeters) on the back of a 90-line carpet, one sees that the rim of a leaf would not be smoothly curved but would move in a stepwise succession. On the back of a carpet this effect remains, but the Chinese weavers eliminate it on the surface of the rug by a technique called "soft-line knotting" or "soft-curving."

This technique is worth describing: the skilled weaver understands that the root of a knot is neither a perfect square nor a circular dot, but an irregular lozenge, its corners overlaid by adjacent knots or lozenges; he manages to tie a knot in the new color at an angle that will overlie a part of the knot in the color tied immediately before, in this manner smoothing the corners of the zigzag into a curve.

This soft-curving technique requires great dexterity on the part of the skilled weaver, and calls into play his artistic talent. Each weaver may produce a flower or leaf different from his neighbor weaver's—one may make the object slimmer and more graceful, the other may make it fuller and plumper—but each will produce a form characteristic of the imagery in Chinese hand-knotted carpets. In addition to the weaver's dexterity and speed in the tying of knots, his skill

and artistry are most important. One of the beauties of Chinese hand-knotted carpets is that each one is slightly different, expressing to some extent the taste and personalities of its weavers.

In their handling of colors the master weavers have developed another specialized technique. The color changes in most hand-knotted carpets are abrupt, without transition. Chinese carpet designs sometimes approximate the brush-drawing effects of watercolor painting, and this requires meticulously graded colors. In depicting scenery a gradual shift of tones is essential to imitate nature's subtleties. Sudden color changes may also be used, according to the requirements of the design. But to capture the delicate tonal variations in the central parts of flowers and leaf veins that deepen from the outside toward the center, for example, special yarns are prepared before the weaving begins. Since each yarn consists of a number of strands, such as 5-ply yarn in the 90-line closed-back quality, each ply or strand may be dyed a different hue and then plied to make yarn in different combinations. This process produces many more shades than could be dyed separately. Yarns color-graded in this manner increase by many times the 600 basic shades available to the Chinese carpet weaver.

Still more sophisticated techniques require great dexterity and attention to detail, such as looping a knot around one instead of both warp strands to create a particular effect. Another special technique in Chinese hand-knotted carpet making produces the "closed-back" and "open-back" methods of

Plates 98 (above), 99 (opposite)
■ *After several months of work, hand-knotted* ■
pile rugs are finished and inspected.

Plate 100
■ *One of the last steps in manufacturing a hand-* ■
knotted pile rug is knotting the fringe.

weaving (see page 154). In the closed-back technique, the usual figure-8 knot is tied around each pair of warp threads after the one in back has been pulled forward; in the open-back technique the knot is tied around each pair of warps without changing the relative position of the forward and rear warps. In both techniques a thin and a thick weft are pounded down after each line of knots has been tied. The closed-back carpet has a harder or stiffer back, the open-back is somewhat more flexible. The two types can be identified by inspecting the carpet back; on the open-back carpet can be seen the white lines of the weft thread. These weft yarns are concealed on closed-back carpets.

SHEARING, LEVELING, AND COMBING THE PILE.

SHEARING, LEVELING, AND COMBING THE PILE. After the hand-knotting process is completed on the loom, the surface must be sheared to a smooth finish. Having tied each line of knots across the entire width, the weaver cuts the pile with scissors to the correct length, usually about one eighth of an inch higher than the finished surface. When the carpet is completely woven, the shearing process starts. With electric shears, craftsmen cut off about one hundredth of an inch of pile on each pass. This is repeated until the correct thickness is reached. The finished shearing produces a perfectly smooth surface, ready for the first sculpturing or incising that is normally done before washing.

The pile yarns are now combed to clear up any tangles that may have de-

veloped in handling the carpet during the tying of knots.

CHEMICAL WASHING OF THE CARPET. This process provides a silky luster and at the same time removes all dirts and fats that may have remained or accumulated in the wool pile. Washing also loosens and straightens the yarns in the pile, increasing the beauty of the work. Chemical washing accomplishes three results:

1. The twisted top of each pile yarn is loosened. The scales on the surface of each fiber are also affected by the washing. As a result the fibers stand erect and in order, and the combination of these factors provides the silky sheen characterizing fine Chinese carpets.
2. As the surplus dyes deposited on the yarns are washed away, the colors take on the lifelike effects intended by the artist.
3. The washing is also insecticidal, killing any larvae that might remain in the wool fiber.

Very old Chinese carpets and other hand-knotted oriental carpets have a silky luster on the surface even though they were not chemically washed when made. Years of walking on the surface with shoes, slippers, or even bare feet eventually imparts a sheen to the wool surface. The longer the carpet has been in use, the higher its sheen or luster is likely to be.

The present method of washing carpets employs the same type of chlorine-based chemicals that were first used in Tianjin in the 1930s. The acids and alkalis used are weak; the chemical reaction is mild and brief. After several chemical treatments, the carpet is rinsed repeatedly in fresh water to free the wools of any residual chemicals. Great care is required to accomplish the beautiful results so admired in these carpets.

SCULPTURING THE CARPET.
The sculpturing of Chinese carpets enlivens the design and creates an effect unique among oriental rugs. Sculpturing draws upon highly trained artists with a keen sense of form and design. There are three steps in sculpturing a Chinese carpet. The preliminary process is called in Chinese *kaihuang* (开荒), literally, "opening up into the wilderness." *Kaihuang* is done between the shearing and the washing: a thin furrow is cut along the general contour of the pattern that clarifies the outlines of the design and lays the foundation for further finishing techniques. "Sloping," *pian* (片) in Chinese, the second step, is also done before washing. A continuous channel is clipped out along the furrowed contours of the objects and sets off the three-dimensional pattern more strikingly. The rug is then sent for chemical washing, rinsed, and dried, and returned to the sculpturing department.

The third and final step is called "incising," *tougou* (投沟) in Chinese, or "rinsing the furrows." With washing and scrubbing the forms woven in the pile have become disfigured to some degree, and the relief produced by the first two steps may have lost its sharpness. A necessary step at this juncture is again to incise the furrows previously opened in order to restore the shapes of the designs, to clarify the outline of the motifs, and to smooth the edges of the furrows.

The Chinese "sculptor" works deftly and at lightning speed, leading the spectator to think his operation is effortless. In fact, his movements require extreme concentration, coordination, and years of training, because a single mistake can ruin months of the weavers' work. This old Chinese craft has now brought the carpet to completion, except for knotting the fringe.

FINAL INSPECTION AND FINISHING THE CARPET.
Every Chinese carpet is meticulously inspected, a process requiring knowledge and skill. The final inspectors are expert in each of the foregoing steps: every carpet and rug is gone over with great care to ascertain that it has been correctly made in every respect, and that no faults are to be found. In the finishing process any irregularities are corrected, if possible; if not, the rug is graded substandard and not shipped as first quality.

The complicated working procedures described here lend superb quality to Chinese carpets. Production is slow: on the average, a skilled worker can tie 6,500 knots on a 90-line carpet in an eight-hour day. This is less than one square foot per day. In the 90-line quality a 9- by 12-foot carpet, measuring 108 square feet, requires six months

Plate 101 (opposite)
■ *A hooking needle threaded with yarn.* ■

Plates 102, 103
■ *A loop-pile hooked rug in preparation.* ■

for a single weaver to complete. A team of four persons weaving (i.e., knotting) such a carpet will need forty-five days to finish the loom work, not counting the hours spent in designing and rescaling, spinning, dyeing, washing, and inspection. These time-honored artistic skills are constantly studied toward improvement and innovation. Carpet craftsmen work together at every stage of production, anticipating one another's needs and suggesting new creative possibilities.

HOOKING. Chinese rug makers have been eager to develop their skills by learning and mastering new techniques introduced to China during the past fifty years. One of these methods, like hand-knotting, relies for success on the dexterity of the human hand to produce a cut-pile or a loop-pile rug that is entirely handmade. The Chinese industry is producing both kinds of carpets successfully.

Making rugs by hooking yarn through a woven backing material was a handicraft created by the colonists in the northeastern part of the North American continent. Their life was hard and it was difficult even to acquire the bare necessities of life. Winters were bitter and houses cold. To keep busy during the cold months when little work could be done outdoors, women developed a technique for making rugs and wall hangings out of strips of old clothing and other woven materials. With the aid of a "hooking needle," they punched each rag strip through an inexpensive woven

material such as, in the old days, burlap or hessian cloth, to create the loop-pile rug called a hooked rug. Various designs were employed, including primitive copies of French Aubusson textile designs, baskets of flowers, geometric forms, and, as skills improved, dogs, cats, horses, and birds. In some areas of New England and Canada, and in other parts of the country as well, women and men still hook rugs —some as a pleasant hobby, some as a small-scale commercial venture. A variant of hooking, "latch-hooking," produces a cut-pile rug with a design that is somewhat less precise than that of a loop-pile rug.

Chinese carpet makers have adopted the Western hooking technique, bringing it to an unprecedented level of mastery. The rug-hooking industry today employs large numbers of workers to craft Chinese wool yarn into cut-pile and loop-pile carpets. A needle is threaded with yarn (Plate 101) and a woven canvas-like cotton material is stretched tightly on a wooden frame to serve as the foundation of the rug, much as cotton warps and wefts create the backing or foundation of a hand-knotted rug. The needle is inserted into the backing (Plate 102), forcing or "punching" the yarn through the cotton; when it is withdrawn, a loop is formed (Plate 103). Using yarn of different colors to produce a design, workers continue the process to complete a loop-pile rug.

To make a cut-pile or "full-cut" rug, the same hooking method is used, but after each loop is punched through the backing material a small scissors-like cutting tool in the needle cuts the yarn (Plate 104). After hooking is completed, the back of the carpet is covered with latex glue and a piece of cotton-scrim to give it strength and stability, and then a fine woven fabric is tacked on over the scrim to provide an attractive finish.

Full-cut carpets made in this manner are finished in the same fashion as hand-knotted carpets: the designs are incised and carved and then the carpet is chemically washed and undergoes a thorough inspection before shipment. Plate 105 shows the handsome product of this technique, which, like hand-knotting, is undergoing continual study and improvement.

---

[1]"Woolen Carpets and Textiles in the Great Yuan" chapter.

Plate 104

■ *The rug shown above can be seen after comple-* ■
tion in Plate 105.

Plate 105 (opposite)

■ *Cut-pile wool carpet made in Tianjin in 1980.* ■
The border contains Buddhist Treasures motifs,
and the central field displays a medley of Con-
fucian and Buddhist symbols, including chess-
board, harp, canopy, umbrella, conch shell, wheel,
and pair of fish. 6' x 9' (1.83 m. x 2.74 m.).

4. MATERIALS

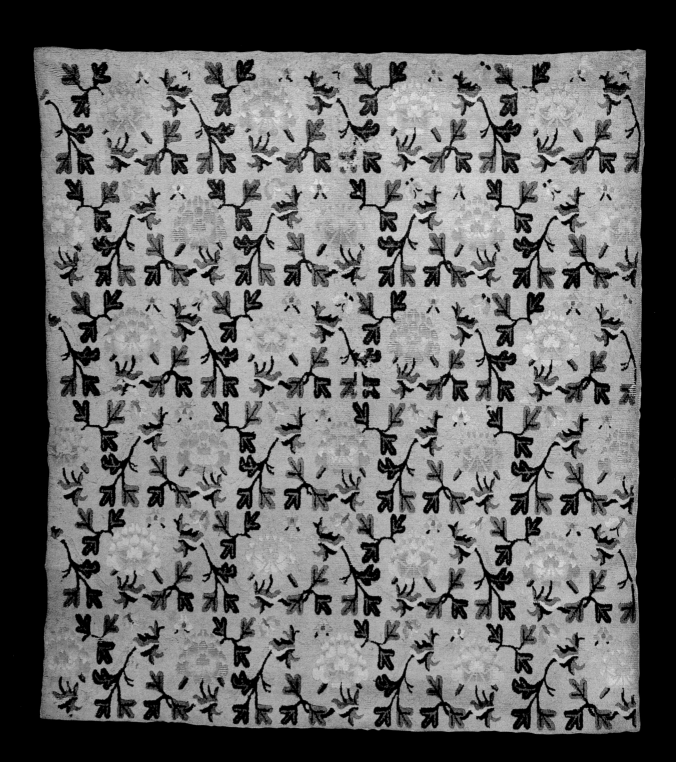

Plate 106
■ *Carpet woven in the nineteenth century. Although it is conceived on a large scale, the all-over* ■
vine and peony design suggests textile patterning. Wool pile; cotton warp and weft; Senneh
knots, 33 per square inch, with Ghiordes knots along left edge; 6' 3½" x 6' 11" (1.92 m. x
2.11 m.). The Textile Museum, Washington, D.C.

Plate 107

Carpet woven in the second half of the nineteenth century. On this wall hanging or pillar cover
two archaic dragons confront each other, striving for possession of a "flaming pearl." The layout
of the design, with a canopy-like top border and an absence of side borders, suggests that this
piece was designed as a pillar cover. Wool pile; cotton warp and weft; Senneh knots, 27.5 per
square inch, with Ghiordes knots along left edge; 5' 8½" x 4' 1" (1.74 m. x 1.25 m.). The
Textile Museum, Washington, D.C. Gift of Jerome and Mary Jane Straka.

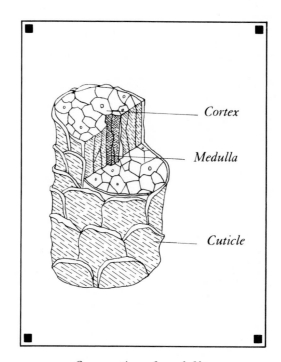

Cross section of wool fiber

The pile or nap of Chinese hand-knotted woolen carpets is made of the finest carpet wool in the world. The yarn comes from long, strong fibers mainly from the wool of mountain sheep. It is tough, resilient, and durable.

The warps and wefts are of sturdy machine-spun cotton yarn; they form the foundation or "backing" of the carpet. Wool was sometimes used for warp and weft in the nineteenth century and before.

Sheep and Sheep Wool

Selecting the wool for carpets is a critical process, for the pile must provide the necessary resilience and toughness, yet its surface must have a silky luster. Not all sheep wool in China is usable for carpet making; the sole source for carpet wool is aboriginal sheep, whose wool is strong, long-staple, and coarse—ideal for the purpose (Plate 110).

The Chinese land mass is vast, stretching from 21° to 53° north latitude. The topography is extremely varied, with high mountains, lowlands, large and small rivers, and lakes. Sheep are abundant in China, but the wide climatic differences produce considerable variations in the type and quality of their wool.

A short description of the structure of sheep wool will help clarify these variations. Microscopic inspection reveals that wool fibers differ in their cellular structure. No sheep grows a fleece composed entirely of one type of fiber. Besides growing pure wool fibers, some sheep, especially the aboriginal types, grow more hairlike fibers and kemp fibers, and whereas pure wool fibers are composed of two sections, hair and kemp have three. The outer section of wool, called the cuticle, is formed of flattened scales that act as a protective covering over the fiber; these scales overlap one another much as fish scales do. The tips of the scales point toward the growth of the fiber and incline slightly outward, giving the fiber a serrated surface that adds to its gripping or locking action in spinning. The scales of coarser wools, each scale being larger and possessing a smooth surface, give forth a stronger reflection of light. That is why coarser sheep wool is more lustrous than finer wool.

The inner section of the wool, the cortex, forms the bulk of the fiber and is made of elongated beanlike cells approximately five times longer than the fiber's thickness. All the physical properties that make sheep wool ideal for carpets—its fineness, strength, resiliency, and color—are produced by the cells of the cortex.

Hair and kemp fibers, besides having a cuticle and a cortex, also have a "medulla" that is corelike in nature. This element accounts for the main differences between those two fibers

Plate 108
Shepherd guarding his flock near the Silk Route town of Karashahr, Xinjiang.

Plate 109
■ *Sheepshearing near Xi'ning, Qinghai.* ■

Plate 110.
■ *Raw wool fiber.* ■

and wool. In China, fiber with two sections only is called unmedullated wool, and it is the finest fiber; fibers with three elements are called either medullated wool, medullated hair, or kemp, and they are coarser. The more developed the medullae, the poorer the quality, and the more easily the fiber will snap or break.

Sheep wools, thus, are sorted into four kinds, with respect to the medullae:

1. unmedullated wool
2. medullated wool
3. heterotype, part wool and part hair; medullae occurring intermittently within a fiber
4. kemp, a heavy, opaque fiber, very brittle owing to overdeveloped medullae and air cavity; does not spin well or dye well

Aboriginal sheep have never been fully domesticated in China, and remain wild in character. The wool fibers of their outer coat have fewer crimps and are thicker in diameter, mostly composed of heterotype, medullated wools. Such fibers are also called hair-like wool. The underlayer of the wool coat has finer fibers with more crimps, mostly unmedullated; these fibers are also called underwool. Kemp fibers occur in wools from certain districts.

Wool is graded by the diameter of the fiber in microns (one micron equals one thousandth of a millimeter):

1. fine wool: diameter less than 25 microns
2. semifine wool: 25 to 34 microns
3. semicoarse wool: 34 to 39 microns
4. coarse wool: 40 to 62 microns

Chinese carpets are made of semifine, semicoarse, and coarse wools.

We can only speculate as to which sheep is the ancestor of all aboriginal sheep in China. Some biologists claim it is *ovis ammon*, the argali "bighorn," or "big head" (*panyang* in Chinese), one of the wild sheep of Asia. A small number of this species still live in the high mountains of northwestern China, now protected by government laws. Breeders were unsuccessful in mating argali sheep with other Chinese aboriginals, and their failure reduces the likelihood of the theory that *ovis ammon* was the earliest ancestor. Other biologists claim *ovis orientalis*, the red sheep (*chiyang* in Chinese), which has rather rust-colored fleece; sheep in southern Xinjiang have fleece with a terra-cotta tinge of color, suggesting a link with the red sheep. Biological investigation shows that the cells of these two distinct breeds have the same number of chromosomes, which supports the hypothesis that Chinese aboriginal sheep were descendants of *ovis orientalis*. There is still too much disagreement to reach a conclusion about which species lies behind the aboriginal sheep of China, however.

Chinese aboriginal sheep are classified into three major breeds, as follows:

MONGOLIAN SHEEP. This species is native to Mongolia and lives on the high plateau in northwestern China. Mongolian herdsmen tribes have inhabited these districts since the early history of the human race in the Far East. Gradually, some tribes moved south to the Yangtze River Valley and the eastern coastal districts, where the more moderate climate favors agricultural production, and as a result these tribes have become distinguishable from those tribes that remained in the north. They brought sheep with them and other animals, all of which propagated and developed in the southern and eastern sections of China. The present Mongolian breed constitutes the largest percentage of aboriginal sheep in China. They are now raised in such widely dispersed provinces and regions as Inner Mongolia, Hebei, Liaoning, Jilin, Heilongjiang, Shandong, Jiangsu, Zhejiang, Anhui, Henan, Hubei, Shanxi, Shaanxi, and Gansu.

Mongolian sheep are raised for both wool and meat. The rams have large horns, the ewes have smaller horns or are hornless; both sexes have broad tails, used to store fat. Their heads are small and narrow, the face-bone curving downward, with expressionless swelling eyes and ears that are generally drooping. Their wools are nearly white. Such sheep are typically coarse-wool bearers, producing medullated (coarse) wool, unmedullated (finer) wool, heterotype wool, and kemp wool. A ram weighs 110 to 155 pounds, a ewe 75 to 110 pounds. Each sheep produces about two pounds of wool annually.

Mongolian sheep have been subdivided into four breeds:[1]

1. Slink sheep, bred in Henan, Hebei, and part of Shandong provinces. Their wool, resilient and crimpy, is among the finest aboriginal sheep wool in China. It is used in the tex-

tile industry as well as in making carpets.

2. Tanyang, or Tibetan lamb, bred in the region of Gansu Province along the Yellow River. This breed is famous for its fur, with a tough but thin pelt and white and lustrous wools. The fibers are soft and crimpy.

3. Dongyang, bred in Shaanxi Province. With its tasty meat and fine white wools, this breed is one of the best aboriginal Chinese sheep, but it is not numerous.

4. Huyang, or Zhejiang lamb, bred in the areas around Lake Taihu in Jiangsu and Zhejiang provinces. These regions have a mild climate, favorable for vegetables and grass. Lambskin is the best-known product from this breed of sheep, used for making gloves and leather jackets. The wool is superior in quality, but since the area around Lake Taihu is a rice-growing region and does not leave much area for pasturage, sheep are bred within enclosures and their buttock and belly wools very often become soiled and stained by excretions; thus, white wools have to be brought occasionally from other regions.

TIBETAN SHEEP. Originally bred on the Tibetan Plateau, these sheep moved gradually to southwest China (Plate 111). Besides Tibet, this sheep is bred in western Sichuan, Qinghai, Yunnan, and Guizhou, in southwestern Gansu, the Hexi Corridor, and the district of the Qilian Mountains. There are two distinct breeds, grassland sheep and valley sheep. Grassland sheep are

Plate 111
■ *Tibetan valley ram.* ■

Plate 112
■ *Kazak ewe.* ■

Plate 113
■ *Kazak ram.* ■

heavier; the ram weighs about 110 pounds, the ewe about 105 pounds. Both sexes have wavy horns, and their wools are mostly white. The valley ram has plump, curved horns with the tips pointing outward; the ewe has a smaller body and no horns. The weight of the ram is 70 to 82 pounds, of the ewe 68 to 79 pounds. Wools from both sexes are white, mostly heterotype wool, resilient and lustrous, ideal for carpet weaving.

KAZAK SHEEP. Bred throughout the region of Xinjiang and in adjacent regions in Qinghai and Gansu provinces, this breed predominates in the Tsaidam Basin region (Plates 112, 113). Thirty percent of the rams and five percent of ewes have horns. The fat tail forms a W shape, emerging undetectably, high above the buttocks, in contrast to the Mongolian sheep's drooping, broad tail. The wool is not all of one color, often a mixture of brown, black, and white; fully white sheep are scarce. The weight of the ram is 132 to 143 pounds, of the ewe, 88 to 121 pounds. The annual output per head is about three pounds of wool, generally not used in carpets because of its variegated colors.

In addition to these aboriginal species, other sheep affording wools for industrial use are Xinjiang sheep, imported species such as Merinos, Corriedales, Lincolns, and some crossbred mutations. But all produce fine or semifine wool, used only in the textile industry, not suitable for carpets. The wools from aboriginal sheep used for carpet making are grouped into the following main types:

XI'NING SHEEP WOOL. Produced in Qinghai Province, the Changdu District in Tibet, the Garze and Aba districts in Sichuan Province and southern Gansu, and the Hexi Corridor, Xi'ning wool comes mainly from Tibetan sheep and from sheep of a Mongolian-Tibetan crossbreed. The chief property of Xi'ning wool is its long fiber (the staple averaging six inches in length) with a balanced proportion of coarse and finer fibers, strong resilience, high tensile strength, good luster, and an off-white color. Xi'ning sheep wool is the ideal material for carpets.

TIBETAN SHEEP WOOL. The special features of this wool produced in the Tibet region, except in its Changdu District, are its whiteness and luster, its excellent resilience, and its long staple. It, too, is an ideal carpet wool, and the Chinese government is improving communication and transportation between the high plateau and inland manufacturing areas so that a greater amount of Tibetan wool will be available in the future.

HEXI SHEEP WOOL. Belonging to the Mongolian wool group, it comes from Ningxia, Gansu, and Shaanxi provinces, the southwest part of Inner Mongolia, and the big bend of the Yellow River. Its special features are off-white color and good luster, and it, too, is excellent material for carpets.

Plate 114

■ *Carpet weaving in Xinjiang. The knots used in this rug-weaving tradition are the same as* ■
those used in the eastern factories of China today, but the looms are still constructed of
wooden timbers.

Plate 115

■ *This carpet, woven in Xinjiang in 1981, is similar in design to Kazak or* ■
Caucasian rugs. Wool pile; cotton warp and weft; Senneh knots; 6' x 9'
(1.83 m. x 2.74 m.).

JINZHOU SHEEP WOOL. Produced in Liaoning and Jilin provinces, this wool belongs to the Mongolian wool group with special features of a grayish white color, good luster, and excellent tensile strength. Occasionally it contains a small amount of kemp wool.

HADA SHEEP WOOL. This is from Mongolian sheep in Jilin, Heilongjiang, and Liaoning provinces. The wool is grayish white in color with medium luster, and it usually contains some kemp wool.

YINGZI SHEEP WOOL. From Mongolian sheep in the central part of Inner Mongolia and Zhangjiakou (Kalgan) in Hebei Province comes this grayish white wool, which has less luster, coarser fibers, and a larger percentage of kemp wool.

HAILAR SHEEP WOOL. Mongolian sheep in northeastern China and in Inner Mongolia produce this wool. The fibers are coarser with poor luster and the wool contains a quantity of kemp.

HUYANG (ZHEJIANG LAMB) SHEEP WOOL. Mongolian sheep in Jiangsu and Zhejiang provinces produce this wool. It is grayish white in color (sometimes stained, see page 175), and has good luster and resilience and little kemp.

The foregoing provides only a general view of the production of aboriginal sheep wools in China. Improvement is ongoing as sheep of superior species are introduced, and the changes for the better that are taking place in the sheep can also be seen in their wool; the amount of wool produced from each cut is increasing. The Animal Husbandry Research Institute is concerned with the requirements of the carpet industry for sheep wool and is attempting to make sure that the aboriginal breeds of sheep will continue to produce wool having strong and coarse fibers, good resilience, good tensile strength, and full luster, thus maintaining the high quality standards of Chinese carpets.

Aboriginal sheep are sheared twice a year. The first cut is taken around March 21, the day called Spring Equinox (春分) in the Chinese agricultural calendar (see Appendix III), and that wool is called spring wool. Spring wool has grown on the body of the animal during the autumn and winter and it contains a large proportion of fine, long fibers, is full of crimps, and has good spinning ability due to its high elasticity. The second cut takes place between Autumn Equinox (秋分), about September 23, and Beginning of Winter (立冬), about November 7; this is called autumn wool. Such wool has grown on the sheep's body during the late spring and summer, when plants and vegetables are luxuriant and plentiful. It contains much heterotype wool, with strong and coarse fibers, high resilience, and elasticity, and it is full of luster. Autumn wool, too, is excellent for making carpets.

Plate 116
■ *Sheep grazing near the Qilian Mountains, Qinghai.* ■

Careful selections from spring and autumn wools are blended by specialists into the wools used in carpet making. The specialists' function is to insure that the wools, when spun into yarns, will possess the three major merits of strength, resilience, and luster.

Other Materials

The overwhelming majority of Chinese pile carpets are made of wool, yet a certain number of carpets are made of silk, jute, flax, goat hair, and synthetic fibers.

Most silk carpets are manufactured in Zhejiang, Jiangsu, and Hebei provinces. It is well known that Zhejiang and Jiangsu, the two provinces at the lower reaches of the Yangtze River, produce the best silk in large quantities. Hebei Province produces its own silk for pile carpet making. In hand-knotted silk carpets today, chrome-dyed silk is always used as the pile fabric; the warps can be either of silk yarn or of cotton yarn, but cotton yarn is almost always used in the weft to give the carpets a stiff foundation.

---

[1]Variations of the original Mongolian species developed through centuries of breeding. They are described today as reservation breeds.

Plate 117

■ *Carpet woven in the late nineteenth century. This is one of a group of rugs with silk pile, metal threads, and an inscription that are believed to have been woven for the Beijing imperial palaces. The inscription on this example translates as "Made for use in the Palace of Eternal Tranquillity." In the field are nine dragons; in the border is the sea and mountain pattern (shoushan fuhai). Silk pile; cotton warp and weft; 4' 2³⁄₈" x 6' 11" (1.28 m. x 2.11 m.). The Textile Museum, Washington, D.C. Gift of Jerome and Mary Jane Straka.* ■

5. IDENTIFICATION AND DATING

Plate 118

■ *Carpet woven in Kashgar in 1981. Central Asian motifs and colors fill this modern rug from Xinjiang. The overall multi-border pattern is reminiscent of the rug shown in Plate 3, woven 150 years earlier. Wool pile; cotton warp and weft; Senneh knots; 4' 3⅛" x 6' 2¾" (1.30 m. x 1.90 m.).* ■

Plate 119

Carpet woven in Baotou, Inner Mongolia, in the early twentieth century. At either end of a circular medallion, garlands of leaves and lotus flowers appear. The main border has a rich ground of natural black wool with patterns of peonies. Wool pile; cotton warp and weft; 2' 4" x 4' 10" (0.71 m. x 1.47 m.). The Textile Museum, Washington, D.C. Gift of Jerome and Mary Jane Straka.

Dating Chinese rugs is a subject of much interest to scholars, collectors, and museum authorities. Although Chinese pile carpets have been collected in the Western world for over one hundred years, knowledgeable people often disagree when they try to date one precisely or even to place it within half a century. In this chapter we try to explain some of the criteria that can be used to determine a carpet's age. We cannot claim to have all the answers, however, and hope that what we have to say will inspire further research and discussion.

Though dating Chinese carpets is not yet an exact science, certain clues may be found in the construction and design of a rug that will indicate an approximate date and place of manufacture. Sometimes it is possible to discover the purpose for which the carpet was intended and sometimes even for whom it was made and his position.

A variety of patterns and weaving techniques were developed during the long history of Chinese carpets and different materials have been used, as well; these are all important factors in determining age. Regional differences in the way people live and special requirements of minority groups can be detected in the diverse sizes, shapes, and patterns of carpets, and these are useful in determining provenance.

Of the oldest carpets available for examination today, few are pre-Ming or even Ming; most were made in the Qing Dynasty. Hand-spun cotton or woolen yarns for warps and wefts, hand-spun woolen yarns for pile, and vegetable dyes were used throughout this long period; thus, we can learn little from the fabric of an ancient carpet unless it contains machine-spun materials, which began to come into use in the 1860s. Moreover, early Chinese writings do not comment directly on workmanship or design, and inscriptions pinpointing the date of manufacture seldom occur on Chinese carpets. Thus, in attempting to date an ancient carpet one must rely chiefly on analysis of its patterns and designs, which also aid in identifying its place of production. With carpets made after 1911, analysis of the fibers and the workmanship are of much greater assistance, for new forms of materials then began to be introduced into the carpet industry in significant quantities.

Yet, in most cases pattern is probably the best guide to identifying roughly the period in which a carpet was woven, the district in which it was produced, the user for whom it was intended, and the purpose it served. When doubt remains, it may prove useful to analyze the warps and wefts, the woolen pile, the dyestuffs, and the weaving techniques. Let us look first at the guidelines of pattern, next at those of workmanship.

In the analysis that follows, three chronological periods in the Chinese carpet industry and three corresponding categories of rugs are referred to:

1. before 1911: "ancient" carpets
2. 1911 to 1937: "old" carpets
3. 1937 to 1983: "contemporary" carpets

Plate 120

■ Nineteenth-century carpet designed for use as a chair back. Woven in the ancient color ■
scheme of dark and light blue on a golden ground, the rug shows archaic four-clawed
dragons over the mountain and sea pattern (shoushan fuhai). An arch of flowering vines
frames the scene. Wool pile; cotton warp and weft; Senneh knots, 49 per square inch;
2' 5⅞" x 2' 6¼" (0.76 m. x 0.77 m.). The Textile Museum, Washington, D.C.

Plate 121

■ Carpet woven in the late nineteenth century or early twentieth century. Even in fragmentary ■
condition this pillar carpet is striking because of its strong color. A five-clawed dragon rears
up against a bright red ground, and other motifs appear in colors of dark and light blue,
purple, ivory, and gold. Wool pile; cotton warp and weft; Senneh knots, 28 per square inch;
4' 4" x 9' 6⅛" (1.32 m. x 2.90 m.). The Textile Museum, Washington, D.C.
Gift of William T. Turner.

The year 1911, the last year of the empire, marked the end of feudalism in China. Before that time industrialization and Western influence had proceeded slowly; Chinese carpets continued to be made in the traditional manner in workshops run in master-disciple fashion, evolving little if at all within a self-sufficient agricultural economy. After the 1911 revolution, China's economy began slowly to improve and in the 1920s foreign buyers, bringing modern entrepreneurial business methods, became instrumental in promoting the sale of Chinese carpets on the international market. Considerable growth subsequently took place in the export of Chinese carpets to Europe and America. Also between 1911 and 1937 imported cotton threads and yarns, aniline dyes, and machine-spinning came into more common use.

During the eight-year Sino-Japanese war (1937–1945), the carpet industry declined as the Japanese tightened the blockade on Chinese business in the coastal regions and forced occupied China to conduct foreign business with Japan alone. Even after V-J day, conditions did not improve, and the carpet industry was unable to carry on production throughout most of China until conditions became more favorable under the government of the People's Republic of China. As we have said, the new government took an interest in Chinese carpet manufacture, seeking out people with experience and knowledge and encouraging them to help the industry eventually to achieve the important position it holds today in the Chinese economy. Thus, in effect, the inaugural date for "contemporary" carpets is 1950.

Patterns

"ANCIENT" PATTERNS. Until the late nineteenth century the carpets made in northwestern China reflected Gansu and Ningxia designs: stylized geometric forms in straight lines woven in yarns dyed yellow, blue, and terracotta. In overall design and in each part, these patterns are symmetrical. During the nineteenth century, European influence was felt in the eastern production centers. Patterns became more complex and motifs denser on the carpet field.

Motifs with auspicious significance always abound in "ancient" carpets. Ming designs have fewer and simpler motifs; Qing carpets became extremely complex, almost fully covered with motifs of symbolic meaning, and the resulting compositions are often overcrowded. The later the date of an "ancient" rug the denser the formations and the greater the number of auspicious motifs. Vegetable and floral patterns are infrequent on Ming carpets, but on Qing carpets narcissus, crabapple blossoms, orchids, and other flowers began to appear. Tide and wave motifs on Ming carpets are gently curving lines; on Qing carpets they are more crimped or curly. During both the Ming and the Qing dynasties, brocades strongly influenced carpet design.

A genuine Ming carpet is a rare sight, but in extant examples geometric brocade-style forms, often with small peach-and-flying-bats motifs, are scattered across the central field. In Qing carpets, this pattern takes another form. Rounded flowers are gathered in groups with two overlapping old coins, on each of which is a bat and a peach, the whole design forming a dense, continuous field.

Peach, pomegranate, and buddha's hand in archaic and modern styles

Ming carpet designs are usually tight and stiff, with simple motifs adapted from the silk-textile industry—Imitation-Song-Dynasty-Brocade or Imperial Warehouse Satin, for example. During the Qing Dynasty, designs became complex, with many borders, flowers in groups that occasionally also include disk forms, and designs filling the corners (Plate 43).

At the end of the Ming and the beginning of the Qing Dynasty (mid-to-late seventeenth century) a simple pattern of archaic dragons lying between *guaizi* (拐子) began to appear on carpets (Plate 29).[1] Archaic dragons in stiff formations gradually gave way to dragons among crockets and tendrils of plants and flowers. This form of the design gradually became the rule (Plate 120).

Another favorite motif on "ancient" carpets, cloud forms are important clues as to the date of a piece. In Ming and early Qing times, clouds are in the form of *ruyi* (Plate 11). In the later Qing, "drifting clouds" became prevalent.

Clouds in ruyi *form*

Drifting clouds

The Ming emperors were protective of Buddhism, probably because the founder of the dynasty had been a Buddhist monk before he commanded the armies that defeated the Mongols. Thus, the Eight Treasures symbols on Ming carpets are usually the Buddhist emblems. On Qing carpets the Eight Treasures are more often Taoist. The Buddhist Eight Treasures on Ming carpets are similar to the Eight Treasures woven into Ming brocades except that the objects are undecorated. On Qing carpets, however, each of the objects eventually acquired characteristic decorations, and with the addition of these secondary elements, the Eight Treasures became the predominant motifs in carpet design. In early Qing

carpets, the Eight Treasures are relatively small in size, nestled among clouds and dragons. In the middle of the Qing Dynasty, after fluttering ribbons had been added, the Treasures assumed an animation that suggests they are floating in space. Lotus seats appear with the Treasures motifs in carpets dating from the end of the Qing (about 1851 to 1911).

Two popular Qing carpet designs are *Bogu* and the Eight Precious Things, miscellaneous treasures that include pearl, coin, lozenge, mirror, horn, and leaf; the musical instrument called a chime stone; and books. Also common on Qing carpets are oblong characters, especially the *shou* in many different forms (see page 127).

The motifs and colors that people were permitted to wear on their robes and other clothing were also used to decorate their carpets. The Ming emperors decreed that the imperial robes were to be made of bright yellow cloth, sewn with golden threads, and embroidered with a round-form dragon having five claws. The dragon is usually seen from the front, with its head looking out from the center of a disk. Princes and princesses of the first and second rank were allowed dragon signs of the same type, but not bright yellow robes, the color reserved for the emperor and empress. Robes of very high court officials of the degree below prince might be decorated with scaleless archaic dragons with four claws. To nobles next in rank and to officials of outstanding service the sovereign granted the right to wear jade-inlaid

The Eight Treasures of Buddhism in archaic and modern styles

Plate 122

■ *"Esthetic" carpets like this one, woven in Tianjin in 1974, have been popular since the* ■
1930s. Based on late eighteenth-century and early nineteenth-century French Aubusson designs,
they reflect the Louis XVI and Empire styles, with symmetrically arranged patterns of flowers
and classical motifs. Wool pile; cotton warp and weft; Senneh knots, 90-line quality; 6' x 9'
(1.83 m. x 2.74 m.).

Plate 123

■ *Carpet woven in Shanghai in 1978. Plum, peony, and crabapple blossoms are scattered across* ■
the field of this rug. Note the soft colors and the fine shading of the flowers. Wool pile; cotton
warp and weft; Senneh knots, 90-line quality; 6' x 9' (1.83 m. x 2.74 m.).

waist belts and robes with a serpent pattern. This creature was given the shape of a dragon but had only three claws. The use of a dragon pattern as an emblem on his household effects by a common person of a grade not yet earned was interpreted as usurpation and brought the death penalty to all his household and blood relatives.

The Qing government followed Ming rules in this matter. The emperors Kangxi and Qianlong, who planned to control the ethnic minorities in China through a policy of conciliation, conferred the titles of dukes, princes, and Living Buddhas on hundreds of Mongolians and Tibetans. These fortunates were also permitted to dress in robes embroidered with dragons designed according to the wearer's degree.

Grand Living Buddhas (the Dalai Lama and his equals) and grand princes (great landowners) were permitted to use carpets and sitting mats decorated with a golden yellow dragon on a light yellow field. The dragon, with white whiskers, green scalp hairs, a white tail, and five claws, was apparently the emperor's dragon, or dragon of the first degree. Second-grade Living Buddhas and princes or dukes of smaller tribal districts were allowed to decorate their carpets, sitting mats, and back cushions with four-clawed blue scaleless dragons on a yellow field. Third-grade minor Living Buddhas and princes or dukes of still smaller tribal districts were to use on carpets, sitting mats, and back cushions, four-clawed blue scaleless dragons on a purple field.

Dragon pattern on rugs produced in Beijing and Tianjin during the 1930s

A number of Grand Lamas, such as the tutors to Banchan Erdini, head-men of Tibetan tribes, regarded with respect as holy creatures between human and fairies, were permitted to use three- or four-clawed scaleless dragons, but no pure yellow was permitted in the field.

At the main prayer halls in the famous Taersi monastery (Stupa Temple) and at the *zhaos* (Mongolian lamaseries) on which an emperor had bestowed his blessing (*bian*, 區),[2] the column or pillar carpets might show dragons with five claws (Plate 121). Those carpets were acknowledged to be the property of the Buddha, not privately owned by any individual. In at least six important lamaseries,[3] the columns are wrapped with carpets showing blue dragons on a field of yellow.

Unlike "old" and "contemporary" carpets woven to the specifications of foreign buyers, "ancient" carpets were made in specific sizes to serve specific requirements. Each piece produced at the end of the nineteenth century in the privately owned workshops in northwestern China was made, depending on function and destination, to precise specifications, as follows:[4]

1. saddle cushions: 2 × 3 *chi* (67 × 100 cm.); 2 × 4 *chi* (67 × 133 cm.); 1.5 × 3 *chi* (50 × 100 cm.)
2. floor coverings for Mongolian yurts: 3 × 5 *chi* (100 × 167 cm.); 3 × 6 *chi* (100 × 200 cm.); 3 × 7 *chi* (100 × 233 cm.)
3. door curtains for Buddhist temples: 6 × 5 *chi* (200 × 167 cm.)
4. seat mats for Grand Lamas: 2.3 × 2.5 *chi* (77 × 83 cm.)

Dragon pattern on rugs made in northwestern China during the Ming and Qing dynasties

199

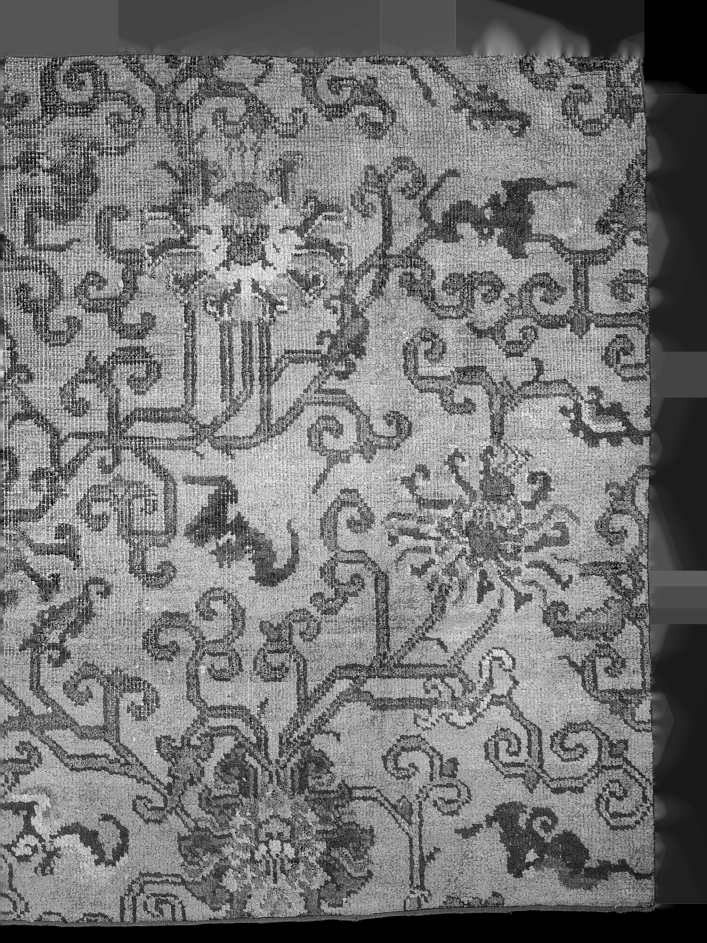

Plate 124

Fragment of a carpet woven in the early nineteenth century. The pattern of the field is domi-
nated by an angularly drawn vine with leaves and stylized blossoms, probably peonies. Bats—
felicitous symbols—also appear in the design. Silk pile; cotton warp and weft; Senneh knots,
63 per square inch; 2' 9⅞" x 4' 4¾" (0.86 m. x 1.33 m.). The Textile Museum, Washington, D.C.

5. prayer mats for disciple lamas: contiguous squares, each 2.1 × 2.2 *chi* (70 × 75 cm.)
6. column or pillar carpets woven to fit, usually 4 *chi* (133 cm.) wide, 7–8 *chi* (233–66 cm.) long
7. carpets woven for the residence of a Living Buddha (those ordered by Grand Lamas, princes, and dukes were of finer workmanship and larger dimensions): 4 × 6 *chi* to 7 × 15 *chi* (133 × 200 cm. to 233 × 500 cm.)

Carpets produced in sets for use in the yurts of Mongolian nobles included ceiling carpets, round-the-wall carpets, and floor coverings, all differentiated by pattern. The round-the-wall carpets are decorated with Buddhist or Taoist Eight Treasures; the ceiling carpets show five bats circling a *shou* character; and the floor carpets have an archaic dragon in a disk on a field of *guaizi* surrounded by a framework of waves.

"OLD" AND "CONTEMPORARY" PATTERNS. During World War I, trade between the Middle East and Europe was severely restricted, and rug importers turned in greater numbers to China. The factories in Beijing and Tianjin were modernized and began to supply carpets in a different style to the West. Most of these included some of the "ancient" design motifs, but the strict symmetry was no longer observed. In the case of the dragon motif, radical changes took place. The laws governing its use were rescinded after the last emperor was dethroned. Suddenly "dragon fever"

spread throughout the country. Gifts passing from Han people to their friends were commonly decorated with dragons. Even the wrapping paper used in grocery stores and confectioneries was printed with five-clawed dragons. Large quantities of dragon carpets were made in Mongolian and Tibetan regions, complicating the dating of all older carpets with this motif. However, "ancient" carpets made to royal order show the whole body of the beast; in more recent carpets clouds often hide some parts of the body, and how to show a dragon coming out of the clouds was governed by new formulas:

1. "three parts seen": head, claws, and a section of the body visible
2. "four parts seen": head, claws, a section of the body, and the tail visible
3. "seven parts seen": head, claws, four sections of the body, and the tail visible

The dragon usually appears in the center of an "old" carpet sometimes rounded into a disk shape. Dragons are also often placed in the four corners of the field (Plate 126).[5]

During the 1920s and 1930s, the patterns of Beijing carpets remained somewhat traditional: a small, round medallion usually lies in the center of an uncrowded field; light-colored borders are filled with traditional motifs such as bat, peony, bamboo, meander, fret, and *wan*. Floral medallions are often rather naturalistic by comparison with earlier examples from the northwestern regions. Tianjin moved farther from tradition, often eliminating the central medallion in favor of asymmetrical designs and naturalistically rendered elements evocative of China: pagodas, Chinese vases, junks, and camel-backed bridges (Plate 77). Many Tianjin carpets of this period are borderless or have a simple border in a single color.[6]

The patterns of "contemporary" carpets include the designs of "ancient" and "old" carpets with alterations according to fashion. Motifs tend to be rounder, smoother, and more realistic in interpretation. Edges lost their zigzag points, colors became softer and more ingratiating (Plate 123).

Phoenix in archaic and modern styles

Plate 125

■ *Antique Finish carpet woven in Gansu in 1978. The central field reproduces an old brocade design. Though there are many motifs, they are held together by a firm geometrical structure and by the repetition of dark blue and apricot in the field and in the wide outer border. Wool pile; cotton warp and weft; Senneh knots; 6' x 9' (1.83 m. x 2.74 m.).* ■

Plate 126
■ *Carpet woven in Shanghai in 1975. In the central medallion is a round-form
dragon, designed according to the "seven parts seen" formula devised after 1911. As
in many "old" carpets, too, dragons also appear in the four corners of the field. The
border displays phoenixes, shous, and the Buddhist Treasures. Wool pile; cotton
warp and weft; Senneh knots, 90-line quality; 6' x 9' (1.83 m. x 2.74 m.)*

Between the mid-nineteenth century and the mid-twentieth century, great changes took place in carpet making, but at different rates in different areas. Just as contact with the West brought much overlapping in the use of old and new designs, Western machine-spun cotton yarns and, later, machine-spun wool yarns did not suddenly replace the hand-spun types. From the 1860s to the 1930s, different materials and methods were in use at the same time in different parts of the country. Some regions were quick to adopt the new yarns, others continued to use the familiar ones. Aniline dyes, too, were not immediately accepted by many producers and buyers for a variety of reasons, including a distrust of new materials and methods, and a reluctance to change. Many may also have preferred the softer shades of vegetable dyes. Thus the presence or absence of modern materials in a carpet is not an entirely reliable measure of its age.

The weaving materials that help to identify the approximate age of a carpet are the warp, the weft, the wool pile, and the dyestuffs. When communications by sea between China and the outer world revived in the 1860s, machine-spun cotton threads and chemical dyestuffs became available, followed by the development of the technique of spinning woolen yarns by machine. The textile industry in China began to change during this period, but for the most part the carpet industry adopted these important materials and techniques somewhat later. Gradually, however, the old-fashioned workshops with their folk-art traditions were replaced by more modern factories using machine-spun thread as warps and wefts as well as chemical dyestuffs.

MATERIALS: WARPS AND WEFTS. Hand-spun thread is easily recognized: irregular twists create a thick strand that is not uniform in cross section. Machine-spun thread is thinner, evenly twisted, and uniform. Statistics of the Chinese Maritime Customs Service show that machine-spun cotton threads were imported from the West as early as the late 1860s. After 1910, factories in the coastal cities, especially Beijing and Tianjin, began to use these 3-ply sewing threads, called "overseas 3-ply" (*yangsan'gu*, 洋三股), as warps, doubling them into cords for strength. After 1920, carpet makers in Inner Mongolia, Gansu, and Ningxia also began to adopt these threads as warps. The wefts were still hand-spun and thin. The use of alternate thick and thin wefts was not yet practiced, and the backs of all carpets were soft.

After 1930, the importation of machine-spun threads increased, spreading from the coastal areas to inland China, and at the same time the Chinese cotton industry also expanded production. Now in factories from Jehol and Suiyuan[7] to eastern Ningxia and Gansu, wefts, too, were made of doubled cords of *yangsan'gu*, two identical wefts being shot through the warps after each line was knotted. However, in the western part of Ningxia, a cotton-growing region, wefts continued to be made of threads hand-spun of local cotton. The use of a thicker weft with a thin weft marked the true beginning of the "contemporary" period, in which the closed-back weaving technique was also developed.

The Chinese carpet industry began to make its own warps and wefts out of cotton fibers after 1950. Four 4-ply 10-count cotton strands were spun into cords for warps, eight 4-ply 10-count cotton strands were used for thick wefts, and one 4-ply 10-count strand was used for thinner wefts. *Yangsan'gu* were no longer needed.

MATERIALS: PILE. As with cotton thread, hand-spinning produces woolen yarn that tends to be uneven in cross section and to have fewer twists; machine-spinning produces woolen yarn with a constant diameter, more twists per inch, and greater tensile strength.

Before 1950, the pile of carpets made in the northwestern provinces, except Ningxia, was usually hand-spun 3-ply or 4-ply woolen yarn. The pile of "ancient" and "old" carpets of 80-line or higher quality produced in the coastal areas is 3- or 4-ply wool yarns. The pile produced in Ningxia is of finer wool and thus is twisted into 4- or 5-ply strands.

Some carpets made in Beijing and Tianjin after 1930 are knotted in machine-spun woolen yarn. After 1950, machine-spun 4- and 5-ply yarns were adopted throughout China, but in some provinces hand-spun yarn continued to be used on occasion.

"Old" as well as "ancient" Ningxia rugs are of Tibetan lamb wool, and the older these carpets are the more glossy they look, even though they have not been chemically washed. In carpets from Suiyuan (Huhehot and Baotou), the region of lamb wool and autumn white wool, the white areas are luxuriant and the pile is soft to the touch. By contrast, carpets from Jehol (Chifeng and Kalgan, now Zhangjiakou) in the east have a rougher pile and are coarser to the touch. The quality of that wool is considered to be second-grade.

Uniformly employed throughout China today for pile are 3.5-count woolen strands twisted into 4-ply yarns for 90-line open-back carpets and 5-ply yarns for 90-line closed-back carpets. A rug with pile of this yarn count is "contemporary," made since 1950.

MATERIALS: DYES. In the coastal areas of Beijing and Tianjin aniline dyestuffs began to be used about 1910, but chemical dyes did not immediately replace vegetable dyes in China; nor did the new chemical dyes make their debut in the form they have today. A period of experimentation took place, and the results were not always fully satisfactory. Aniline dyes, which impart a reddish tinge to a carpet, were applied, with mixed results. Some workshops tried to blend chemical with vegetable dyes, first applying a vegetable dye bath—yellow, for example—then a chemical dye to obtain a particular color. Finally, they decided that chrome dyes produced the best results and gave up the use of vegetable dyes in the 1930s.

Differences in composition between vegetable and chemical dyes are detectable by spectrometric analysis. If spectrometric equipment is not available, certain visual tests may be conducted.

Only indigo blue, terra-cotta red, black, tan, purplish red (from sumac), bright lemon-yellow and golden yellow, and fugitive yellowish green vegetable dyes were made in ancient China. No bright green or violet blue existed. Chemical dyes, on the contrary, exist in a full range of colors and hues, including the absolute colors of red and green, which cannot be produced from plant sources.

The hues of vegetable dyes are distinctive, too, to the practiced eye of a connoisseur or experienced buyer. For example, pink has a violet hue; deep red has a dominant tinge of iron rust; indigo blue, after long exposure to light and air, develops a blue-black appearance and sometimes has a tinge of green.

Except for blue and pink, vegetable colors are obtained by dyeing first with yellow, then with another, stronger shade, which nevertheless retains a yellowish hue.

Of all the color areas in "ancient" carpets, the indigo blue are the most resistant to wear; no vitriol is added to the dye bath and the structure of the wool is unharmed (Plate 30). Wool dyed black or tan is less tough because vitriol or the dye itself has weakened the yarn. Indeed, though the black and tan yarns of an "ancient" carpet may be worn out, the blue may remain comparatively fresh and unworn. All color areas of chemically dyed woolen pile rugs usually wear down at the same rate.

Creating a full range of colors by twisting together strands of different hues is a recent development. The practice was begun after 1920 in eastern factories and it gradually spread westward. Baotou craftsmen accepted it first, followed by the workshops of Shaanxi, Ningxia, and Gansu.

TECHNIQUES. "Ancient" carpets of northwestern origin are open-backed, with uniform pairs of wefts. In the "old" northwestern products woven in Yulin (Shaanxi Province), every tenth weft is red. In Ningxia and Gansu, carpets sometimes have woolen wefts, and in such cases there are fewer warp lines. The density of a carpet's warps and wefts is also a clue to its place of origin. Generally speaking, in the carpets made in the former province of Suiyuan at the end of the nineteenth century, the number of knots in the horizontal and the vertical directions are the same. A number of "ancient" carpets with hand-spun cotton warps and wefts originating in the western part of Ningxia do not have equal numbers of knots in the two directions. In each square *chi*, the number of warps is greater than the number of wefts (in one instance, 90 pairs of warps, 70 pairs of wefts).

No cutting was done on "ancient" rugs; the first incised carpets date from the late 1920s. In the "contemporary" period sculpturing and embossing were added to the carpet makers' repertory (Plate 55).

General Remarks

Carpets of 80-line quality and higher are common in most monasteries and lamaseries. Those used in ordinary homes are usually of 80-line quality or lower. Carpets used by important persons, including Living Buddhas, have as many as 120 lines per foot, closely knotted with the best woolen yarns. The patterns of such carpets are fine and delicate. Carpets for *kangs* in the houses of peasants and herdsmen, and carpets for saddle covers are made with less skill and are of about 70-line quality.

Some carpets woven with vegetable-dyed yarns, whose patterns are old-fashioned or roughly executed, are not necessarily "ancient." The warps tell the real story: if they are of imported *yangsan'gu* threads, the carpet was produced during the transitional period when both vegetable and chemical dyes and both hand-spun and machine-spun yarns were used. Such rugs would probably be between seventy and eighty years old.

Carpets with old-style patterns, made with imported cotton warps and chemically dyed woolen yarns, belong to the "old" category. They may have been woven to the order of Mongolian or Tibetan nobles according to deliberately selected old-fashioned designs. Old-style patterns in rugs dyed with "three blues" vegetable dyes, but with smooth, elastic curves, probably date relatively early in the "old" period and come from northern Shaanxi, for weavers in that region were the first to perfect curved lines in their patterns.

Workshops in eastern Inner Mongolia (Jehol or Chahar[8]) accepted machine-spun cotton thread and chemical dyes earlier than those of the western part of Suiyuan. In both areas during the "old" period, carpet patterns remained old-fashioned.

For carpets of better quality (90-line and up) woven in northwestern China, imported cotton threads were adopted and used earlier than for lower quality. But the opposite holds true for the adoption of chemical dyes. The northwestern craftsmen considered imported machine-spun threads to be superior to the indigenous hand-spun product but imported dyes to be inferior to vegetable dyes.

These are the features of a genuinely "ancient" carpet (produced before 1911):
patterns as described on pages 193–94, 198–99, 202
hand-spun wool pile
hand-spun cotton warps and wefts, or wool wefts, of equal thickness
open-back construction
vegetable dye colors

Carpets with the following features are "old," produced between 1911 and 1937 in the northwestern provinces:

patterns as described on pages 202–3
hand-spun wool pile or (possibly) machine-spun wool pile
machine-spun cotton *yangsan'gu* warps or (possibly) hand-spun cotton warps
hand-spun cotton wefts, or (possibly) machine-spun cotton wefts, of equal thickness
open-back construction
vegetable or (possibly) aniline dye colors
pile may be incised but not embossed

Carpets with these features are "old," produced between 1911 and 1937 in the coastal regions:

patterns as described on pages 202–3
hand-spun wool pile or (possibly) machine-spun wool pile
machine-spun cotton *yangsan'gu* warps or warps of other cotton material
hand-spun cotton wefts, or (possibly) machine-spun cotton wefts, of equal thickness
open-back construction or (possibly) closed-back construction
chemical dye colors or (possibly) vegetable dye colors
pile may be incised and/or embossed

Carpets with these features are "contemporary," produced after 1937:

patterns as described on page 203
machine-spun wool pile
machine-spun cotton warps
machine-spun cotton wefts, one thick and one thin
open-back or closed-back construction
chemical dye colors (but see below)
incised and/or embossed

An incised and embossed carpet with a traditional design of the Ming or Qing dynasties; with machine-spun cotton warps and wefts; and with machine-spun pile is "contemporary," treated with a special wash and called Antique Finish. Since 1979 or 1980, most of these rugs have been dyed with vegetable colors (Plate 125).

---

[1] A *guaizi* is a bilaterally symmetrical motif used as a center ornament or, halved, as a corner ornament.

[2] Denoted by a large nameplate hung in a conspicuous location.

[3] Xilitu Zhao (Yan Shousi), in Huhehot, Inner Mongolia; Xilamulin Zhao (Tunghuisi), in Siwangzigi, Inner Mongolia; Bailingmao, in Inner Mongolia; Zunger Zhao, in Dongsheng, Inner Mongolia; Fushouxumeisi, in Chengde, Hebei Province. These *zhaos* and Taersi in Qinghai Province were the most important lamaseries in China.

[4] One *chi* equals 33.3 centimeters; conversions are given in round figures. See Appendix II.

[5] A carpet design having a central medallion and a pattern repeated at the four corners is jokingly called *sicai yitang* (四菜一汤), "dinner with soup and four courses." This is the way the table is generally set in the average home in central and southern China.

[6] For this description of "old" rugs woven in eastern China, we are indebted to Alix G. Perrachon's interesting article, "The Vogue of the Chinese Carpet: The Peking and Tientsin Era," *Hali*, vol. 5, 1982.

[7] In 1954 the Chinese province of Suiyuan was incorporated into Inner Mongolia; in 1956 the province of Jehol was broken up and in part absorbed by Hebei and Liaoning provinces.

[8] In 1954 Chahar Province was broken up and incorporated into Hebei and Shanxi provinces.

APPENDIX I: THE CHINESE CLASSICS

Certain books of a doctrinal nature written in ancient times and later published collectively with notes and exegesis by Confucian scholars are regarded as classics in China. The first compilation, published during the Zhou Dynasty, incorporated five works, called the Five Classics. They were republished during the Song Dynasty along with other works as the Thirteen Classics. Associated with the Confucian tradition, they were required subjects of study for every student and scholar who sought to win an official appointment by passing government examinations.

The Thirteen Classics

Zhouyi (Book of Changes) deals with prediction and divination.

Shangshu (Documents from High Authority) is a collection of official statements from the royal archives of the Shang and Zhou dynasties.

Maoshi (Book of Odes, edited by Mao Chang) contains poems and songs of the Shang and Zhou dynasties.

Zhouli (Rituals of Zhou) records the ritual practices of the imperial Zhou household.

Yili (Rituals of the Eastern Zhou) records the ritual practices and regulations of the royal and aristocratic houses during the Spring and Autumn Period and the Warring States Period.

Liji (The Rituals) is a selection of essays concerning ritual practices before the Han Dynasty.

Chunqiu Zuo Zhuan (History of the Spring and Autumn Period, edited by Zuo Qiuming) is a collection of narratives of historical events based on an outline by Confucius.

Chunqiu Gongyang Zhuan (History of the Spring and Autumn Period, edited by Gongyang Shou) is another collection of narratives of historical events based on the same outline by Confucius.

Chunqiu Guliang Zhuan (History of the Spring and Autumn Period, edited by Guliang Chi) is another collection of narratives of historical events based on the same outline by Confucius.

Lunyu (Analects of Confucius) contains answers to a series of questions compiled by Confucius's disciples.

Xiaojing (Code of Filial Piety) instructs children how to behave toward their parents.

Erya (Dictionary of Words) was the first Chinese dictionary.

Mengzi (Analects of Mencius) is a philosophical work compiled by Mencius (Mengzi) and his followers that develops Confucian thought.

APPENDIX II: CHINESE MEASUREMENTS

The Chinese unit of length has been an interesting concept since early times. That unit is called *chi* (尺), and before the twentieth century all carpets produced in China were measured in *chi*. For this reason, the length and width of old carpets and rugs are rarely divisible by feet or meters.

Chi has no invariable standard as a base, as does the meter, which is one ten-millionth of the distance from the North Pole to the Equator as measured along the meridian that passes through Paris; the measurement of *chi* has varied during China's long history.

The *History of the Han Dynasty* describes how the length of *chi* was established. It says that in the earliest days a grain of glutinous millet *(panicum miliaceum)* was chosen to furnish an objective length, called *fen* (分) and one hundred *fen* make one *chi*. Since a grain of millet is not a perfect sphere, the method of lining up one hundred grains was disputed: some insisted that the grains be aligned vertically, with the short axis along the line, others preferred using the long axis. More-over, millet grains may differ in size depending on several factors—the species and its growing conditions, including soil, climate, and water.

In excavations of ancient relics, archaeologists have often found different scales and rulers for measuring. During the Han Dynasty *chi* measured between 22 and 23 centimeters; during the Tang and Song dynasties *chi* grew, until about 1000 A.D. it measured about 32 centimeters. Since governments in those days levied taxes in kind on lengths of silk, linen, and cotton, the *chi* grew longer in order to collect more taxes. The longest *chi* we know is almost 37 centimeters.

During the 1930s the Chinese government proclaimed a "1-2-3" system that linked Chinese measurements with the metric system. One *sheng* (升), the Chinese basic measurement of volume, came to one liter; two *jin* (斤), a measurement of weight, equaled one kilogram; and three *chi* became specified as one meter (3.28 feet). The "1-2-3" system is the standard today for measuring volume, weight, and length.

APPENDIX III: CHINESE CALENDARS

China has two calendars. The official one is the Gregorian solar calendar used in most countries. The other is a lunar agricultural calendar, in which occasionally a year has thirteen months. Such a year is called a *runnian*.

This lunar calendar is actually based on the movements of both sun and moon. Each month has either 29 or 30 days, and the moon is full on the fifteenth day of each month. The Chinese lunar year has only 354.3672 days, whereas the more accurate Gregorian calendar year has 365.2422 days. To make up the difference, the ancient Chinese astrologers invented a way of interpolating 7 additional months of 29 days each into each 19-year period. When an intercalary month occurs is determined by the position of the sun in the zodiac.

There are 24 seasonal days in the Chinese lunar calendar. Twelve mark the sun's entry into one of the segments or "houses" of the zodiac; twelve mark the sun's arrival at the midpoint of a segment or house. The places of these days in the lunar calendar change every year, but in the solar year they fall on about the same day in successive years. The equinoxes, solstices, and seasonal days are regulated by the 24 solar periods, which average about 15 days each.

CHINESE (LUNAR) CALENDAR

Seasonal Days	Sun's Position in the Zodiac	Approximate Date in the Gregorian (Solar) Calendar
Beginning of Spring	Aquarius midpoint	February 6
Rain Water	Pisces threshold	February 20
Excited Insects	Pisces midpoint	March 6
Spring Equinox	Aries threshold	March 21
Clear and Brightness	Aries midpoint	April 5
Grain Rains	Taurus threshold	April 20
Beginning of Summer	Taurus midpoint	May 6
Grain Fills	Gemini threshold	May 21
Grain in Ear	Gemini midpoint	June 6
Summer Solstice	Cancer threshold	June 22
Slight Heat	Cancer midpoint	July 7
Great Heat	Leo threshold	July 23
Beginning of Autumn	Leo midpoint	August 8
Limit of Heat	Virgo threshold	August 23
White Dew	Virgo midpoint	September 8
Autumn Equinox	Libra threshold	September 23
Cold Dew	Libra midpoint	October 8
Frost Descents	Scorpio threshold	October 24
Beginning of Winter	Scorpio midpoint	November 7
Little Snow	Sagittarius threshold	November 22
Heavy Snow	Sagittarius midpoint	December 7
Winter Solstice	Capricorn threshold	December 22
Little Cold	Capricorn midpoint	January 6
Severe Cold	Aquarius threshold	January 20

APPENDIX IV: A NOTE ON *PINYIN*

Pinyin, or to be exact, *hanyu pinyin* is the new system for writing Chinese Han characters in the Latin alphabet, adopted officially on 1 January 1979 by the People's Republic of China. Invented by the Chinese, *hanyu pinyin* has been widely used for years in China in commercial establishments, as well as in elementary textbooks of the Chinese language as an aid in learning the Chinese Han characters.

Since the Middle Ages, when Europeans first became aware of China, Chinese names for persons, places, and things have been converted into numerous foreign languages. Based on the foreigners' best pronunciations of Chinese, many different spellings developed. Among these, the Wade-Giles system of romanization, published in 1867 by Thomas Francis Wade, a British diplomat at the Beijing Manchu court, became the most widely used. The Wade-Giles system was based on the Brit-

ish pronunciation of words. *Hanyu pinyin*, which more closely approximates the actual sounds of the Chinese language, has replaced such traditional romanization systems as Wade-Giles for personal names and other words and the Postal Atlas system for place names.

Chinese characters are the same all over the country and their meaning is the same, but they are pronounced differently in different localities. To make it possible for people all over China to understand one another, *pu'tonghua*, the Mandarin dialect spoken in Beijing, is taught in schools throughout the People's Republic of China. The *pinyin* system is based on *pu'tonghua*.

In this book, with a few exceptions, the *pinyin* system is used for ancient and contemporary Chinese names. Below are a number of proper names in *pinyin* and Wade-Giles/Postal Atlas.

Pinyin	*Wade-Giles/Postal Atlas*
Altai	Altai
Anhui	Anhwei
Bo Juyi	Po Chü-i
Ban Chao	Pan Ch'ao
Ban Gu	Pan Ku
Banpo	Panp'o
Baotou	Paot'ou
Beijing	Peking
Changdu	Ch'angtu
Changjiang (Yangtze R.)	Ch'angchiang (Yangtzechiang)
Chengdu	Ch'engtu
Chifeng	Ch'ih-feng
Cixi	Tz'u-hsi
Cui	Ts'ui

Pinyin	*Wade-Giles/Postal Atlas*
Datong	Tatung
Dongsheng	Tungsheng
Dou Xian	Tou Hsien
Du Fu	Tu Fu
Dunhuang	Tunhuang
Facun	Fa Ts'un
Gansu	Kansu
Gaozu	Kao-tsu
Guangzhou	Canton (Kwangchow)
Guizhou	Kweichow
Guo Moruo	Kuo Mo-jo
Haojing	Kaoking or Haoking
Hebei	Hopei
Heilongjiang	Heilungkiang
Henan	Honan

Pinyin	Wade-Giles/Postal Atlas	Pinyin	Wade-Giles/Postal Atlas
Hetian	Hotien (Khotan)	Sui	Sui
Hexi	Hohsi	Suiyuan	Suiyuan
Huanghe	Huangho	Suzhou	Soochow
(Yellow R.)		Taiyuan	T'aiyüan
Huangzhong	Huangchung	Taizong	T'ai-tsung
Hubei	Hupei	Tang	T'ang
Jiangsu	Kiangsu	Tian	T'ien
Jilin	Kirin	Tianjin	Tientsin
Jin	Chin	Tongzhi	T'ung-chih
Jingdezhen	Ching-te-chen	Urumqi	Urumchi
Kangxi	K'ang-hsi	Wei	Wei
Kong Qiu	Kung Ch'iu	Wudi	Wu-ti
Kunlun	Kunlun	Wutaishan	Wu-t'ai-shan
Lanzhou	Lanchow	Wu Zetian	Wu Tse-t'ien
Laozi	Lao-tzu	Xia	Hsia
Liaoning	Liaoning	Xi'an	Sian
Liu Bang	Liu Pang	Xiang Yu	Hsiang Yü
Luoyi	Loyi	Xianyang	Hsienyang
Lu You	Lu You	Xing	Hsing
Ming	Ming	Xi'ning	Sining
Mingdi	Ming-ti	Xinjiang	Sinkiang
Mingfeng	Mingfeng	Xiongnu	Hsiung-nu
Modi	Mo-ti	Xuan Zang	Hsüan Tsang
Ningxia	Ninghsia	Xuanzhou	Hsüanchow
Qiang	Ch'iang	Yangshao	Yang-shao
Qianlong	Ch'ien-lung	Yin	Yin
Qilian	Ch'ilien	Yinchuan	Yin-ch'uan
Qin	Ch'in	Yiyuan	Yi-yüan
Qing	Ch'ing	Yuan	Yüan
Qinghai	Ch'inghai	Yunnan	Yünnan
Qin Hui	Ch'in Hui	Yuezhi	Yüeh-chih
Shaanxi	Shensi	Zhangjiakou	Chang-chia-k'ou (Kalgan)
Shandong	Shantung	Zeng Qianyuan	Cheng Ch'ien-yüan
Shang	Shang	Zhao	Chao
Shanghai	Shanghai	Zhejiang	Chekiang
Shanxi	Shansi	Zheng Zhong	Cheng Chung
Shihuangdi	Shih-huang-ti	Zhongzong	Chung-tsung
Sichuan	Szechwan	Zhou	Chou
Song	Sung	Zhuangzi	Chuang-tzu
Songjiang	Sungkiang	Zunhua	Tsunhua
Su Dongpo	Su Tung-p'o	Zuo Zongtang	Tso Tsung-t'ang

Guide to Pronunciation

The letters of the *pinyin* and Wade-Giles romanizations approximate in pronunciation the italicized letters in the words in the "equivalent" column.

Pinyin	*Wade-Giles*	*equivalent*
f	f	*f*ee
h	h	between *h*ot and I*ch* (German)
l	l	*l*ad
m	m	*m*ight
n	n	*n*o
r	j	between *r*ust and *j*eune (French)
s	s, ss, sz	*s*eat
x	hs	between *s*eat and *sh*eet
w	w	*w*alk
b	p	*b*ought
p	p'	*p*ie
d	t	*d*ot
t	t'	s*t*arling
g	k	*g*old
k	k'	*c*ut
c	ts', tz'	po*ts*
z	ts, tz	pa*ds*
j*	ch	*g*in
zh*	ch	*j*olt
q*	ch'	*ch*eap
ch*	ch'	*ch*alk
sh	sh	*sh*oe
y	y	*y*oung
a	a	h*a*rd
ai	ai	p*ie*
an	an	w*an*t, except after *y*
yan	yen	between *yen* and *yank*
ang	ang	*Ang*st (German)
ao	ao	cl*oud*
e	e	between tak*e*n and d*u*n
e	e	*o*ff, after *h*, *k*, *k'*
ei	ei	*ei*ght
eng	eng	s*ung*
i	i	between d*i*n and d*ea*n, except after *s*, *ss*, *sz*, *sh*, *ch*, *ch'*, *zh*
(s)i	(ss)u	hidd*en*
(sh)i	(sh)ih,	
(ch)i	(ch')ih,	b*urr*
(zh)i	(ch)ih	
ia	ia	*ya*cht
ian	ien	between *yen* and *yank*
iang	iang	h*e* + *ang*
iao	iao	y*ow*l
ie	ieh	*ye*n
in	in	between *in* and d*ean*
ing	ing	s*ing*
iong	iung	*jung* (German)
iu	iu	between *you* and L*eo*
o	o	*o*ff
ong	ung	*jung* (German)
ou	ou	s*ew*
ou	u	s*ew*, after *y*
u	u	*too*
u	ü	d*u* (French), after *j*, *q*, *y*, *x*
ua	ua	*wa*nt
uai	uai	*wi*ne
uan	uan	*wan*t
uan	üan	d*u* (French) + *yan*k, after *j*, *q*, *y*, *x*
uang	uang	*wan* + *x*ing
ui	ui, uei	*weig*h
ue	ueh	d*u* (French) + *ye*t
un	un	between *un*der and *Owen*
uo	o, uo	t*owa*rd

*Pinyin *j* and *zh*, *q*, and *ch* are not distinguished in Wade-Giles transcription but differ in pronunciation: *j* and *q* are "dry" sounds, pronounced with tongue flattened against the upper palate; *zh* and *ch* are "wet," spoken with the tip of the tongue curled up to touch the upper palate.

APPENDIX V: TIME CHART

China	B.C.	Elsewhere in the World
Yangshao Age (Neolithic cultures)		Neolithic cultures in eastern Europe, Mediterranean area, Near East, and India
	3500	
	3100	Old Kingdom in Egypt 3100–2258
Bronze Age begins		Bronze Age begins in Aegean area and Near East
	2700	Early dynastic cultures in Mesopotamia
	2500	Neolithic cultures in Japan
Xia Dynasty 21st century–17th century	2000	Aryans invade India 2000–1500
	1900	First Dynasty of Babylon 1894–1595
Shang Dynasty 17th century–11th century	1700	
	1600	New Kingdom in Egypt 1570–1085
	1400	Mycenaean Greek culture at its height 1400–1200
		El Amarna period in Egypt c. 1375–1360
	1100	Greeks begin to colonize Ionian coast of Asia Minor
Zhou Dynasty 　Western Zhou 11th century–771	1000	King Solomon rules in Jerusalem 970–931
Eastern Zhou 770–221	800	First Olympic Games held in Greece 776
		Traditional founding of Rome 753
Spring and Autumn Period 770–476		
	700	Babylon sacked by Assyrians c. 689
		Assyrians invade Egypt 673
Laozi born end 7th century		Traditional founding of Japanese state 660
	600	Prince Siddhartha, Gautama Buddha, born in India c. 563
Confucius born c. 551		Roman Republic founded 510
	500	Greeks defeat Persians at Salamis 480
		Socrates (469), Plato (c. 427) born in Greece
Warring States Period 475–221		
	400	Aristotle born in Greece 384
Mencius born 372		Alexander the Great succeeds to throne of Macedon 336
	300	Emperor Asoka reigns in India c. 273–232
First recorded use of compass c. 250		First and Second Punic Wars 264–241, 218–201
Qin Dynasty 221–207		
Han Dynasty 　Western Han 206 B.C.–24 A.D.		

	200	
Yuehzhi migrate westward into Tarim and Ili basins (170–160), into Transoxiana (140–135), establishing Kushan Dynasty in northwestern India (c. 50)	100	Defeat of Carthage by Rome, 146
		Julius Caesar dictator of Rome 49–44
		Roman Empire established 23
		Jesus Christ born in Judaea 8–4
	A.D.	
Eastern Han 25–220		Conquest of Britain by Rome 43–44
Invention of paper c. 100	100	Roman victory brings Armenia, Mesopotamia, and Assyria as new provinces into the empire 117
	200	Artaxerxes (Ardashir) becomes ruler of Sassanid Empire in Persia 224
Three Kingdoms: Wei (220–65), Shu (221–63), Wu (222–80)		Celebration of millennium of Rome 248
Jin Dynasty Western Jin 265–316		
	300	Edict of Milan: Christianity becomes tolerated throughout the Roman Empire 313
Eastern Jin 317–420		Division of Roman Empire into eastern and western branches 395
Southern and Northern Dynasties (Six Dynasties). 420–589	400	Fall of the West Roman Empire 476
		Clovis establishes Frankish Empire 486
	500	Justinian restores hegemony of Rome in Mediterranean 527–65
		Khosru I (Chosroes) brings Sassanid Empire to its greatest extent 531–79
Sui Dynasty 589–618		Mohammed born in Mecca 570
Tang Dynasty 618–907 Xuan Zang makes pilgrimage to India and back 629–45	600	
		Taika Reforms transform Japanese government into a replica of the Chinese 646
		Umayyad caliphs reign in Damascus 661–750
Woodblock printing in use by 700	700	Nara Period in Japan 710–84
Invention of gunpowder 8th century		Byzantine emperor Leo III stops Arab advance westward 718
		Abbasid caliphs reign in Baghdad 762–836
	800	Charlemagne crowned emperor of the West 800
		Three-way partition of Carolingian Empire 843
		Fujiwara Period in Japan 857–1160

Five Dynasties (907–60) and Ten States (907–79)	900	Normandy awarded to Vikings by king of France 911
Song Dynasty 960–1279		German king Otto I founds what will become Holy Roman Empire 962
		Hugh Capet (r. 987–96) founds Capetian Dynasty in France
	1000	
Invention of movable type 1044		William of Normandy conquers England 1066
		Byzantines crushed by Turks at Manzikert 1071
		First Crusade 1095–96
Southern Song Dynasty 1127–1279	1100	
		Henry II becomes first Plantagenet king of England 1154
Government issues paper money 1189		Yoritomo establishes military dictatorship in Japan 1185
	1200	
Genghis Khan becomes ruler of all the Mongols 1206		Fourth Crusade conquers Constantinople 1202–4
		Magna Carta limits power of English kings 1215
Yuan Dynasty 1279–1368		Marco Polo travels to China 1271–95
Guo Shoujing invents highly accurate solar "time-service calendar" 1281		Moslems conquer Acre, last Christian stronghold in Holy Land, 1291
		Osman I (r. 1299–1324) establishes Ottoman (Turkish) Empire
	1300	Exile of papacy at Avignon 1309–78
		Japan divided into southern (Yoshino) and northern (Kyoto) dynasties 1336–92
		Hundred Years' War between France and England begins 1337
Ming Dynasty 1368–1644		
		Ashikaga (Muromachi) shogunate reunifies government in Japan 1392
Seven great maritime expeditions take Chinese fleet as far as Africa 1407–35	1400	
		Constantinople conquered by Ottoman Turks 1453
		Henry VII (r. 1485–1509) first Tudor king of England
		Hapsburgs rule Holy Roman Empire 1493–1806
		Spain and Portugal divide New World 1493–94
	1500	Martin Luther outlawed and excommunicated 1521
		Mogul Dynasty founded in India 1526
		Suleiman the Magnificent, emperor of Turks, threatens Vienna 1529

Li Shizen compiles illustrated pharmacopoeia describing 2,000 drugs and giving 8,000 presciptions 1590	1550	Spanish Armada defeated by English 1588
		Hideyoshi reunites all Japan 1590
	1600	Tokugawa shogunate founded in Japan by Ieyasu 1603; shoguns adopt "closed-door" policy toward Europeans 1633–39
		First European settlement in America at Jamestown, Va., 1607
		Romanov Dynasty rules Russia 1613–1917
		Thirty Years' War in Europe 1618–48
Qing Dynasty, 1644–1911	1650	Protectorate in England under Cromwell 1653–58; monarchy restored 1660
Zheng Chenggong (Koxinga) expels Dutch from Taiwan 1662		Louis XIV absolute ruler of France 1661–1715
	1700	Peter the Great (r. 1682–1725) westernizes Russia
	1750	
		First British governor general of India appointed 1774
		American Revolution 1775–83
		French Revolution 1789–99
		Consulate of Napoleon 1799–1804
	1800	Revolution in Latin America brings independence to Spanish colonies 1822
First Opium War 1839–42		Queen Victoria crowned 1837; empress of India 1877
		Revolution of 1848 in Europe
	1850	Fall of Tokugawa shogunate in Japan. Meiji Restoration 1868
		U.S. Civil War 1861–65
		Franco-Prussian War 1870–71; Bismark first chancellor of German Empire
	1900	Russo-Japanese War 1904–5
China is a Republic 1912–49		World War I 1914–18
		Bolshevik Revolution 1917
Sino-Japanese War 1937–45		Spanish Civil War 1936–39
		World War II 1939–45
		British rule ends in India 1947
People's Republic of China founded 1949	1950	Korean War 1950–53

BIBLIOGRAPHY

Chinese-language Sources

Chen Bangzhan. *Chronicles of the Song Dynasty*. Ming Dynasty.

Ennin. *Diary of a Pilgrimage to Tang China in Search of the Law*. 4 vols. Tang Dynasty, c. 848 A.D.

Fan Ye. *History of the Later Han Dynasty*. Song Dynasty.

Feng Chengjun. *Gazetteer of the Western Lands*. Beijing: Zhonghua Bookstore, Ltd., n.d.

Ge Hong. *The Life of the Emperor Wudi of the Han Dynasty*. Jin Dynasty.

Jian Bozan, Shao Xunzheng, and Hu Hua. *A Concise History of China*. Beijing: Foreign Languages Press, 1964.

Marvelous Things in the South. Ming Dynasty.

Polo, Marco. *Travels*. Trans. Feng Chengjun. 3 vols. Beijing: Zhonghua Bookstore, Ltd., 1954.

Ren Jiyu, comp. *History of Chinese Philosophy*. Beijing: People's Publishing House, 1966.

Sima Qian. *Historical Records*. Han Dynasty, c. 85 B.C.

Tao Zongyi (Tao Nancun). *A Sketchbook Written in My Spare Time after Working in the Fields*. Yuan or Ming Dynasty. c. 1350–1400.

Xiao Ai. *History of Bone Inscriptions*. Beijing, 1980.

Xiu Ouyang. *History of the Tang Dynasty*. Song Dynasty.

Yang Sheng. *Sketchbook by Sheng An*. Ming Dynasty. Repr. Beijing: Zhonghua Bookstore, Ltd., 1977.

Zhang Xinglang, comp. *Materials on Intercommunication between China and the West*. Beijing: Commercial Press, Ltd., 1930.

English-language Sources

Campbell, Joseph. *The Masks of God: Oriental Mythology*. New York: Penguin Books, Inc., 1962.

Christie, Anthony. *Chinese Mythology*. London: Hamlyn Publishing, Ltd., 1968.

Cohen, Joan Lebold, and Cohen, Jerome Alan. *China Today and Her Ancient Treasures*. 2d ed. New York: Harry N. Abrams, Inc., 1980.

Dilley, Arthur Urbane. *Oriental Rugs and Carpets*. New York: Charles Scribner's Sons, 1931.

Fung, Yu-lan. *A Short History of Chinese Philosophy*. Ed. Derk Bodde. New York: Macmillan Publishing Co., Inc., 1948.

Goodrich, L. Carrington. *A Short History of the Chinese People*. 3d ed. New York: Harper and Row Publishers, Inc., 1959.

Hall, Manly P. *The White Bird of Tao*. Los Angeles: Philosophical Research Society, Inc., 1964.

Jenyns, Soame. *A Background to Chinese Painting*. New York: Schocken Books, Inc., 1966.

Lorenz, H. A. *A View of Chinese Rugs from the Seventeenth to the Twentieth Century*. London and Boston: Routledge & Kegan Paul, Ltd., 1972.

Okakura, Kakuzo. *The Awakening of Japan*. New York: Century Co., 1905.

Perrachon, Alix G. "The Vogue of the Chinese Carpet: The Peking and Tientsin Era." *Hali*, vol. 5, 1982.

Stein, Sir Aurel. *On Ancient Central-Asian Tracks*. New York: Random House, Inc. (Pantheon Books), 1964.

Sullivan, Michael. *Chinese and Japanese Art*. London: Grolier, Inc., 1965.

The World's Great Religions. New York: Time-Life Books, 1955.

INDEX

Page numbers in *italic* type refer to illustrations.

Photo Credits

Photographs have been supplied by the authors, except as specified below. Numbers refer to plates.

Metropolitan Museum of Art, New York: 2, 11, 21, 28

Yasuo Muro: 23, 46, 54

Tsugusato Ohmura: 108

Seigo Ohtsuka: 13, 16 (photo), 20, 114

Royal Ontario Museum, Toronto: 1, 15, 36, 41, 45, 67, 68

Textile Museum, Washington, D.C.: Frontispiece, 3–5, 7, 29, 30, 34, 35, 37, 38, 42, 43, 47–50, 52, 53, 57, 60, 66, 69, 71, 72, 78, 79, 81, 106, 107, 117, 119, 120, 121, 124

The map on pages 38–39 is adapted from *China Business Review*, published by the National Council for U.S.-China Trade, Washington, D.C.